Oxford University School of Archaeology
Monograph 33

DIGGING NUMBERS
ELEMENTARY STATISTICS FOR
ARCHAEOLOGISTS

(Second Edition)

Mike Fletcher and Gary Lock

Oxford University School of Archaeology
2005

Published by
Oxford University School of Archaeology
Institute of Archaeology
Beaumont Street
Oxford

© Mike Fletcher and Gary Lock 2005

First published 1991
reprinted 1994, 2001, 2004
Second edition 2005, reprinted 2006

ISBN 0 947816 69 0   978 0 947816 69 8

A CIP record for this book is available from the British Library

This book is available direct from
Oxbow Books, Park End Place, Oxford OX 1 1HN
(Phone: 01865-241249; Fax: 01865-794449)

and

The David Brown Book Company
PO Box 511, Oakville, CT 06779, USA
(Phone: 860-945-9329; Fax: 860-945-9468)

and

via our website
www.oxbowbooks.com

Printed in Great Britain by
Antony Rowe Ltd., Chippenham

CONTENTS

Preface

Section 1: Techniques for describing and presenting archaeological data

Section 3: Books and software

Preface (First Edition)

Note on the contents list: we have intentionally tried to produce user friendly headings to try and overcome the problems inherent in statistical beginners being faced with a list of technical names. This has resulted in a considerable amount of simplification which may offend some statistical purists. We beg understanding in advance.

Digging Numbers comprises four sections;

Section 1. Simple techniques for describing and presenting archaeological data,
Section 2. Techniques for drawing inferences from archaeological data,
Section 3. An introduction to statistical computing,
Section 4. A catalogue of selected statistical packages.

The first two sections are sequential in the sense that Section 2 assumes familiarity with the concepts and techniques covered in Section 1.

Section 1 starts with a discussion of the structure and organisation of archaeological data-sets which are suitable for statistical analysis. It introduces a hypothetical data-set which describes measurements and other aspects of forty bronze and iron spearheads. This data-set is used throughout Sections 1, 2 and 3 to demonstrate the different statistical techniques and concepts. Chapter 2 outlines a statistical approach to analyzing such a data-set. It assumes familiarity with Chapter 1 and is meant to act as a guide through the rest of Sections 1 and 2.

The rest of Section 1 is concerned with what are usually called Descriptive Statistics. These include several methods of displaying the distribution of a single variable in tabular and pictorial form as well as simple ways of displaying the relationship between two variables. Measures of position (usually thought of as 'the average') and measures of dispersion or variation (the 'spread' around the average) are also described. All of these are applied to the spearhead data-set.

Section 2 outlines the main types of Inferential Statistics. These involve the concepts of Sampling, Probability, Hypothesis Testing and Statistical Significance. Some of the more commonly used Tests of Difference, Tests of Distribution and Tests of Association are described and illustrated with examples from the spearhead data-set.

In Sections 1 and 2 statistical formulae are stated and used without derivation or proofs. This is due to limited space and mainly to the fact that this book is aimed at people with little or no statistical knowledge. It is felt that most users will be prepared to accept a formula as stated. If statistical derivation is required appropriate books are recommended in Chapter 12. References throughout the text are to the few recommended books described in Chapter 12, there is no formal bibliography.

The emphasis here is on using the appropriate technique and understanding the results in both statistical and archaeological terms. Where applicable, this includes working through examples by hand (with a calculator). This may seem a little old-fashioned in todays world of computers but we feel that the benefits in understanding are well worth the effort.

Even so, many people will have access to a computer and this is where Sections 3 and 4 comes in. Most of the techniques described in Sections 1 and 2 have one or two corresponding computer programs listed in Section 3. These are written in SPSS and Minitab.

Section 4 is a catalogue of commercially available statistical packages. This gives details of hardware requirements, the software's contents and availability and includes general packages as well as specific archaeological software.

This combination should allow the user of Digging Numbers to approach statistical analysis either by calculation by hand, or by using a commercial software package. Although the two packages we have chosen to demonstrate are relatively expensive ones (SPSS and Minitab), many of those listed in Section 4 are inexpensive with some being available as Shareware.

It is probably already apparent that this book provides only an introduction to the complex world of statistics. There are whole areas of statistical reasoning and analysis which are not even mentioned. Many different methods of multivariate analysis, for example, have proved to be of importance to archaeologists. Even so, statistics seems to be one of those subjects that can cause instant mental paralysis in many otherwise competent archaeologists. If this book can give someone enough confidence to approach a more advanced text then our aim will have been achieved.

Throughout the book three icons are used to quickly highlight either a reference in Chapter 12, a link with another chapter or a program number from Section 3.

Acknowledgements.
We would like to thank Clive Orton of University College London for his meticulous reading of an earlier draft of this book. His detailed comments were of great help to us. Thank you also to Hazel Dodge for being a guinea-pig, to all the suppliers of software for Section 4 and to H.R. Neave for permission to use some of his statistical tables. Any mistakes or misunderstandings that remain in the text are the responsibility of the authors.

Simon Pressey drew the cover illustration.

Technical note: camera-ready copy for this book has been produced by the authors using Timeworks Desktop Publisher. Figures have been produced using Gem Graph and Gem Draw and integrated electronically. We would be happy to discuss this process with any interested parties.

GRL and MF, February 1991.

Preface (Second Edition)

Over the last thirteen years or so we have been pleased by the continuing popularity of Digging Numbers as an introductory text for archaeologists wanting to get started with statistics. Several people and organizations have requested that we update it and so, after a series of reprints of the First Edition, here is the Second Edition.

The underlying philosophy and much of the text remains the same. This is still an introductory book that is meant to get people doing statistics for themselves within a basic understanding of the strengths and limitations of various techniques. There are, however, several important changes within the Second Edition:

1. A new chapter (12) has been added which provides an introduction to multivariate techniques. The emphasis of the book is still on descriptive and inferential techniques but this new chapter gives a taste of what can be done using more than one or two variables.
2. Section 4 of the First Edition, the catalogue of statistical software, has been omitted as it is no longer relevant.
3. Chapter 13, recommended books, has been re-written and updated.
4. Chapter 14, computer programs, has been completely re-written. This Second Edition uses SPSS for PC and many of the figures within the text are SPSS output so that text and figures are more closely linked.

We would like to thank the many people who have contacted us about Digging Numbers over the years, especially those who have pointed out errors and typos, not least Philip Balcombe. We have attempted to rectify them all but please do get in touch if any remain. Thank you also to Barry Cunliffe for encouragement and Val Lamb of Oxbow Books for guidance.

GRL and MF, January 2005.

CHAPTER 1

AN INTRODUCTION TO DATA

1.1 The Example Data Set

It is important that any data set to be used for statistical analysis be well organised and properly defined. This often results in a rectangular block of numbers which is called a **data matrix**. Table 1.1 is a data matrix with 40 rows and 14 columns, or a 40 by 14 matrix (downloadable from http://www.soc.staffs.ac.uk/mf4/spears.zip).

Table 1.1 describes forty spearheads. Each horizontal row represents one spearhead and is, therefore, one **item** in archaeological terms. In statistical terms this is referred to as one **case** (often one **record** in database terminology). Each vertical column represents one observation on the item and is, archaeologically speaking, one **attribute**. In statistical terms this is a **variable** (equivalent to a **field** in many database applications).

There are fourteen variables in Table 1.1. The first one is a label in the form of a unique number for each case; this is essential for any form of cross-referencing with other information about the spearheads. Each variable has a **variable name** which is displayed at the top of the column.

From now on variable names that refer to the spearhead data-set are enclosed in < >.

1.2 Levels of measurement.

Variables can be measured at one of four levels. This classification was first introduced in 1946 and has become universally accepted by statisticians. As will become apparent during this and the next section, it is important to know at what level variables are measured. Many statistical techniques can only be applied to variables at a certain level of measurement or higher. The four levels are, in ascending order; nominal, ordinal, interval and ratio.

NOMINAL (in name only). Nominal variables consist of categories which have no inherent ordering or numeric value. Each category is assigned an arbitrary name. In Table 1.1 the following variables are nominal;

<MAT>, <CON>, <LOO> and <PEG>

NUM	MAT	CON	LOO	PEG	COND	DATE	MAXLE	SOCLE	MAXWI	UPSOC	LOSOC	MAWIT	WEIGHT
1	2	3	1	2	3	300	12.4	3.1	3.6	1.0	1.7	6.2	167.0
2	2	3	1	2	4	450	22.6	7.8	4.3	1.3	1.6	11.3	342.1
3	2	3	1	2	4	400	17.9	5.2	4.1	1.7	2.0	7.5	322.9
4	2	3	1	0	4	350	*	*	*	1.4	2.0	*	154.8
5	2	3	1	1	3	350	16.8	6.6	5.7	1.1	1.7	7.0	358.1
6	2	3	1	2	3	400	13.3	3.1	4.1	1.6	1.9	5.6	227.9
7	2	3	1	2	2	450	14.1	5.8	5.8	1.2	1.8	6.8	323.8
8	2	2	1	2	4	600	*	6.1	5.9	1.3	1.7	7.1	285.2
9	2	2	1	2	4	150	22.5	9.2	6.2	1.3	2.0	13.1	613.8
10	2	1	1	2	3	300	16.9	4.5	3.6	1.4	1.9	5.2	254.3
11	2	1	1	2	2	50	19.1	4.6	4.1	1.5	1.8	10.6	310.1
12	2	1	1	2	3	100	25.8	8.6	4.7	1.4	1.6	12.7	426.8
13	2	1	1	2	2	600	22.5	8.4	3.9	1.7	2.7	18.0	521.2
14	2	1	1	2	3	300	27.6	8.7	6.0	1.5	2.1	14.4	765.1
15	2	1	1	2	2	350	38.0	9.6	5.6	2.0	2.6	13.6	1217.2
16	2	1	1	2	2	350	72.4	14.4	6.4	2.0	2.4	17.6	2446.5
17	2	1	1	2	2	350	37.5	10.2	3.9	1.8	2.1	14.1	675.7
18	2	2	1	2	3	450	10.2	3.0	2.7	1.4	1.5	5.8	90.9
19	2	2	1	2	2	200	11.6	4.6	2.0	0.9	1.7	5.6	86.8
20	2	2	1	1	3	400	10.8	3.1	2.7	1.9	1.7	5.4	109.1
21	1	1	2	1	2	900	11.4	4.2	1.8	0.8	1.5	6.1	67.7
22	1	1	1	2	2	900	16.6	7.2	2.8	1.6	2.0	9.5	204.5
23	1	1	2	1	1	1000	10.2	3.4	3.3	1.9	2.3	5.4	170.3
24	1	1	2	1	1	1200	18.6	6.6	2.7	1.4	1.6	8.5	176.8
25	1	1	2	1	2	1200	24.4	7.5	4.4	1.7	2.3	11.3	543.2
26	1	1	2	1	1	1000	23.5	8.0	4.5	2.0	2.7	8.7	628.2
27	1	1	2	1	2	1200	24.8	8.1	3.5	2.0	2.1	11.1	401.0
28	1	1	1	2	1	800	14.1	3.4	3.9	1.7	2.5	6.1	302.4
29	1	1	1	2	2	800	24.6	6.0	4.8	2.1	2.4	8.6	623.5
30	1	1	2	1	2	800	30.9	5.1	6.0	1.5	2.4	8.0	978.9
31	1	1	1	2	1	700	20.2	5.9	5.7	1.7	2.4	9.4	607.9
32	1	1	1	2	2	700	12.8	3.5	2.8	1.5	2.1	5.9	165.6
33	1	1	1	2	1	800	16.9	5.5	3.6	1.6	2.3	8.2	307.9
34	1	1	1	2	1	800	14.2	4.3	2.8	1.3	2.2	6.0	192.4
35	1	2	1	2	2	700	18.0	4.5	5.3	1.6	2.5	9.9	524.7
36	1	1	2	1	2	1000	11.7	3.6	2.4	2.2	1.8	6.6	111.2
37	1	1	1	2	1	800	14.1	5.4	2.4	1.5	2.4	8.4	178.7
38	1	1	2	1	2	1200	17.7	4.8	3.9	1.2	1.8	9.6	273.4
39	1	1	2	2	3	1200	36.6	13.5	6.0	1.6	2.7	18.1	1304.4
40	1	1	2	1	2	800	12.3	2.4	5.4	1.1	1.6	7.2	233.8

Table 1.1. The spearhead data-set.

Column	Variable Name	Description	Values
2	<MAT>	Material	1 = Bronze
			2 = Iron
3	<CON>	Context	1 = Stray find
			(inc. hoards)
			2 = Settlement
			3 = Burial
4	<LOO>	Loop	1 = No
			2 = Yes
5	<PEG>	Peghole	1 = No
			2 = Yes

For each of these variables there is no significance in the values '1', '2' and '3' that have been assigned to the categories (i.e. '2' is not twice the value of '1'), any other numbers or names would do. Note that it is good practice to avoid the use of 1 for 'yes' and 0 for 'no' as this can confuse the distinction which often needs to be made between 'no' and 'no information' (or 'missing data').

ORDINAL (forming a sequence). Ordinal variables also consist of categories but this time they have an inherent ordering or ranking. There is, however, no fixed distance between the categories. The only ordinal variable in Table 1.1 is column 6 <COND> which has the following values;

1 = Excellent   2 = Good   3 = Fair   4 = Poor.

Here we can state the relationship of '2' as being between '1' and '3' but it is wrong to assume equal distance between categories as is implied by the numeric values.

It is possible that a nominal variable could become ordinal if an ordering is imposed by a typology although this will be based on some external criteria and is not inherent within the data.

Some statistical tests will accept a dichotomous nominal variable (one with only two categories) as being ordinal. Many dichotomous variables are presence/absence variables; they record whether the attribute is there or not. Care must be taken when dealing with missing values which can be frequent in archaeological data. Spearhead Number 4 has missing values (indicated by *) for variables 8, 9, 10 and 13 because it is badly damaged and those measurements can not be taken. It can be confusing to represent missing values with a numeric value such as 0.0 or 99.9, choose something obvious such as *. Missing values can cause complications in presence/absence data. The value 'absent' is different to 'not known' (if the relevant piece of information can not be measured) and a third category may have to be introduced; Present Absent and Missing.

INTERVAL (a sequence with fixed distances). An interval variable has the properties of an ordinal variable with the added property that the distances between the values can be interpreted. A popular way of explaining this concept is to look at methods of measuring temperature. The values 'hot', 'warm', 'cool', and 'cold' are ordinal because the difference between 'hot' and 'warm' and the difference between 'warm' and 'cool' are not defined. A temperature of 30°C is not only higher than one of 20°C but it is 10°C higher. The interval is meaningful, therefore temperature Celsius is an interval scale.

The only interval variable in Table 1.1 is column 7 <DATE>. If we take spearhead numbers 9, 10 and 18 they have the dates 150BC, 300BC and 450BC respectively. The difference in years between Number 18 and Number 10 is the same as between Number 10 and Number 9. It is obviously incorrect, however, to interpret Number 10 as being twice as old as Number 9 even though this is implied by the numeric values of '300' and '150'. With interval variables there is no meaningful datum or zero.

RATIO (fixed distances with a datum point). This is the highest level of measurement with the properties of interval data plus a fixed zero point. If the dates mentioned above were converted to a new variable <AGE> so that a value of '1,000' was twice as old as '500' this would then be a ratio variable. Returning to the measuring of temperature, 20°C is not twice as hot as 10°C because 0°C is not a datum point, it does not imply no heat. Temperature in degrees Kelvin, on the other hand, are measured on a ratio scale because 0°K does mean no heat and 20°K is twice as hot as 10°K.

In Table 1.1 columns 8 to 14 inclusive are all ratio variables. They are metric measurements as shown in Figure 1.1.

It is also quite common to refer to nominal and ordinal variables as **categorical** (or **discrete**) variables and to interval and ratio as continuous variables. The variable values of categorical variables are usually chosen by the analyst and because this can be a fairly arbitrary process these are sometimes referred to as **qualitative** variables. The values of continuous variables tend to be more objectively arrived at and these are sometimes called **quantitative** variables.

Just because nominal variables are classified as the lowest level of measurement their importance within archaeology must not be underestimated. Some fundamental archaeological concepts involve the use of nominal data, the processes of classification and typology are important examples.

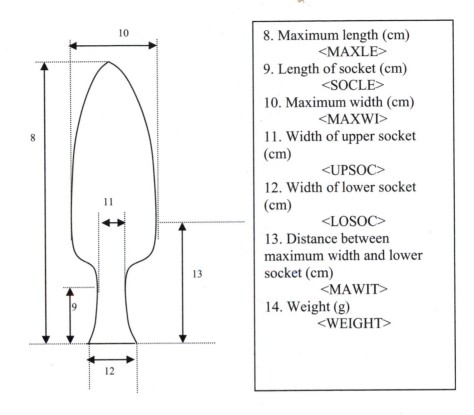

8. Maximum length (cm) <MAXLE>
9. Length of socket (cm) <SOCLE>
10. Maximum width (cm) <MAXWI>
11. Width of upper socket (cm) <UPSOC>
12. Width of lower socket (cm) <LOSOC>
13. Distance between maximum width and lower socket (cm) <MAWIT>
14. Weight (g) <WEIGHT>

Figure 1.1 The seven quantitative variables.

All observations involve a level of **accuracy**, especially on continuous variables. The level of accuracy decided on must be adequate as a basis for sensible decisions and interpretations during analysis. Variables 8 to 13 in Table 1.1 are all recorded to the nearest millimetre, to be any more accurate is unnecessary although not physically impossible. Once data have been collected no amount of statistical manipulation will improve their accuracy.

1.3   Coding

With categorical variables it is necessary to represent the values of the categories in a standardised way by using a **coding system**. It is common in statistical analysis to use a numeric coding system, in fact, using letters rather than numbers can cause problems with some statistical software. All of the categorical variables in Table 1.1 have values represented by a unique **integer** number. This is easy to process but is obscure because the meanings of the code have to be remembered or looked up, if the data set is large and/or complex this can be very time consuming and become a major drawback with numeric coding. Another problem with this method is the potential for a higher error rate in the data and the associated problem of error coding.

Obscurity (and thus many errors!) can be reduced by using an **abbreviated keyword** coding system. In such a system the values of the variable <CON>, for example, could be represented by the code 'str', 'set' and 'bur'. For complete clarity a **full keyword** code would use the values 'stray find', 'settlement' and 'burial'. Both keyword systems can create more work during data recording although the extra time spent typing can be offset by not having to look up codes. Codes containing letters (alphanumeric) can cause problems with some software; make sure to check first!

Whatever coding system is used it must be exhaustive and exclusive. Exhaustive in that every possible data value is catered for and exclusive because every value will only fit into one category. Each observation must fit into one and only one category of the coding system (even if it is a category called 'miscellaneous' for those values that don't fit elsewhere).

1.4   Transforming variables

Table 1.1 shows the observations as recorded, these are the raw data. It is sometimes useful to transform one or more of the original variables to create new variables for analysis. Transformations can involve a single variable or be a relationship between two variables.

GROUPING. Values of a continuous variable can be grouped to create a new categorical variable. The variable <DATE> could be chopped up into the three values '1200 to 650', '649 to 100' and 'after 99' to create the new variable <PERIOD>. The values of <PERIOD> would be 'Later Bronze Age', 'Earlier Iron Age' and 'Late Iron Age' and could be used for the basis of establishing changes in the spearheads through time. Performing statistical analyses on each of the three groups of <PERIOD> could identify temporal trends.

The grouping of continuous variables is flexible in that new groups can be created to suit a particular analysis. This is a useful technique for exploring a data-set. If data for many more spearheads became available it may prove interesting to divide <PERIOD> into more than three categories for finer temporal investigations.

Although grouping of continuous variables can be very useful it must be remembered that it involves a loss of information. It is always better to record data as a continuous variable and then group, rather than to record initially as a categorical variable.

RATIOS. Sometimes the relationship between the values of two variables can express a new attribute of interest. By performing a calculation on the two values the new attribute can be stored as an extra variable. This usually applies to continuous variables.

As an example, the ratio between the two variables <MAXLE> and <MAXWI> will express something of the overall shape of the spearhead. Short, wide spearheads will have a different value to long narrow ones. The ratio can be calculated by dividing <MAXLE> by <MAXWI> as follows;

Spearhead number	<MAXLE>	<MAXWI>	Ratio <LE/WIRAT>
1	12.4	3.6	3.4
39	36.6	6.0	6.1

The difference in overall 'shape' is expressed in the two values of the ratio for spearheads 1 and 39.

It is now possible to use the two new variables <PERIOD> and <LE/WIRAT> to investigate temporal trends in the shape of spearheads. It is often the case that as exploration of a data-set progresses so new ways of expanding the original variables by creating new ones are thought of. It can be informative to 'play' with the data, to explore relationships and see if the results are interesting.

Another measure of some aspect of shape could be a proportion stated as a **percentage**. A good example is to take the length of socket as a proportion of the maximum length by dividing <SOCLE> by <MAXLE> and multiplying by 100 as follows:

Spearhead number	<SOCLE>	<MAXLE>	Proportion
1	12.4	3.1	0.25 (25%)
22	16.6	7.2	0.43 (43%)

Percentages are often used to measure frequencies or counts but can be deceptive unless the raw counts are also given.

Points to remember:
However a variable is measured, mm, g, %, years etc. it is essential to state clearly the **units** used for this measurement and, as far as possible, to use a consistent set of units. Do not mix mm. with inches!

Always keep a copy of the original data. As an analysis progresses the data being used can change in form. If a computer is being used it is very easy to overwrite old versions of data with new versions.

Keep a record of any changes made to data. It is very easy to lose track of how an analysis has developed. If the results are to be published it is important for other workers to have access to the original data and to be aware of how the data have been altered.

CHAPTER 2

A STATISTICAL APPROACH – SIGNPOSTING THE WAY

We are now in a position to be able to record data in a suitable format for statistical analysis. This chapter outlines a general statistical approach which can be applied to any data-set while, at the same time, it attempts to guide the reader through the following chapters. It is useful to preserve the two stages implied by the structuring of this book: the initial descriptive and exploratory stage and then the inferential stage when hypotheses can be formally tested. Going beyond these relatively simple techniques it may then be suitable to apply multivariate techniques to try and understand more complex patterns within the data.

The descriptive and exploratory stage (Chapters 1, 3, 4 and 5).
The suggested approach is meant to emphasise the exploratory nature of statistical analysis. The aim is not to perform 'an analysis' to produce 'the answer' but rather to execute successive passes through the data gradually identifying trends and patterns that look interesting and can be followed up by further investigation. A series of sequential steps can be recommended, of which the first two have already been described.

Step 1 (Chapter 1).
Establish the structure of the data.
- Assign variable names, identify the level of measurement for each variable.
- Assign a case identifier if there is not one.
- Decide on the coding of nominal and ordinal variables.
- Decide how to code missing values.

Step 2 (Chapter 1).
- Produce a rectangular data matrix aligning the columns.
- Visually scan the matrix for any obvious errors.

Step 3 (Chapter 3).
- Investigate the gross values of each variable individually (i.e. univariate analysis). This is still primarily screening for errors. It is important to be sure that the data are absolutely error free.
- The minimum and maximum values of each variable can be initially important in identifying possible errors. For categorical variables using a numeric or alphanumeric code this can show cases of gross misclassification. For continuous variables this can show errors of measurement (although it could be a genuine outlier).
- Correct any errors and repeat this step.

Step 4 (Chapters 3, 4 and 5)

Investigate the distribution and parameters of each variable (still univariate) using the full range of descriptive statistics.

- For categorical variables the most useful will be frequency tables, bar charts and the modal value(s).
- For continuous variables the mean, median, range and standard deviation together with histograms, stem-and-leaf plots, boxplots and ogives will probably be the most productive.
- Use pictures and graphical techniques wherever possible, these can be much more informative than numbers alone.
- Investigate the same variable several times over – don't just produce one result and claim it is 'the answer'. For example, if a continuous variable is being analyzed by a histogram or stem-and-leaf plot, use several values for class intervals and midpoints and compare the results.
- Create new variables by transformations (Chapter 1) and repeat step 4.
- Anomalies and errors in the data can still be identified at this stage. Correct any and return to step 3.

This is the end of the basic analysis and error checking procedures.

Step 5 (Chapters 3, 4 and 5)

Certain simple, albeit often important, archaeological questions will have been answered during step 4, these will have been univariate in nature i.e. concerning the distribution and other characteristics of a single variable. The minimum, maximum and average weight of spearheads, the numbers of spearheads from different context types are such questions. The next stage of archaeological questioning will involve some kind of comparison of two variables: bivariate analysis.

It is here that the intuitive nature of statistical analysis becomes more important because control is in the hands of the analyst: the analysis should be archaeologically driven. On the one hand statistics are just a tool capable of providing answers to archaeological questions but the real power of statistics is that they can be more than that – statistics can trigger new approaches to a data-set, generate new questions, and it is this that makes the intuitive, iterative nature of a statistical analysis important.

Bivariate questions involve comparison of some kind and form the basis of much archaeological analysis. Comparisons will probably be one or more of the following:

- **Comparison using two categorical variables** (including grouped continuous variables). This is a contingency table approach (Chapter 3), an example being material of spearhead by find context.
- **Comparison using one categorical variable** (including grouped continuous variables) **and one continuous variable** (Chapters 3, 4 and 5). This approach produces statistics for the continuous variable, using the techniques as in Step 4, for each category of the categorical variable and compares them. A simple example would be a histogram, mean and standard deviation for the maximum length of spearheads from each category of find context – how do they compare?

It is quite common in both of the above comparisons for one of the categorical variables to be either time or position related. This results in the investigation of temporal and spatial trends respectively – the two most important lines of enquiry in archaeology.

- **Comparison using two continuous variables**. A scatterplot of the maximum length by the maximum width of the spearheads is an example.

It is important to realise that:

- **All three methods of comparison could include data from another data-set**, comparing data from two different sites or areas for example. How does the maximum length of our spearheads compare to the maximum length of those from a different area?
- **All three methods of comparison can be developed to include techniques of formal inference and hypothesis testing**. Is there a statistically significant association between the material of the spearheads and their find context or could it have happened by chance? Is the relationship between the maximum length and width of the spearheads significant?

The answering of such questions involves the concepts of probability theory and statistical significance and move us into the second stage.

The inferential stage (Chapters 6 to 11)
Chapters 6 and 7 provide the underlying theory for the techniques involved in drawing inferences from the data. Both should be read before attempting anything described in Chapters 8 to 11.

It is important to realise that moving into the inferential stage is not an essential step, the methods described above form the basis of many an excavation report or research paper. The difficult part of a statistical analysis is often the initial posing of the archaeological question in statistical terms. This has been compared with translating between two different languages: archaeology has its own theoretical language and statistics has an operational language. Once the translation has been done, and it is clear just what relationship between which variables represents the archaeological question to be answered together with which statistical technique is needed, it could be that one of the descriptive methods will provide enough information.

There is a general move in statistics away from rigid confirmatory approaches (i.e. one analysis produces 'the answer') towards a much more flexible exploratory approach, this applies to inferential techniques as well as descriptive methods.

It has already been stated that some of the descriptive techniques mentioned above form the basis for inferential statistics. Distribution characteristics such as the variance and the mean can be tested (Chapters 8 and 9), as can relationships displayed by scatterplots (Chapter 10) and contingency tables (Chapter 11). In every situation, however, it is important to remember just what it is that is being tested, i.e. it is the **statistical significance**. This is a very different thing to **archaeological significance** and the two should not become conflated. We may identify patterns within the data that are statistically significant at the 95% level but unless this can be translated back into the theoretical language of archaeology, and be given meaning in archaeological terms, it will not be archaeologically significant. Another problem, which again can only be answered in archaeological terms, is that of which level of statistical significance is really meaningful. If something is statistically significant at the 90% level but not at the 95% level what does this mean in archaeological terms? Is it important? Statistical analysis of archaeological data should not be reduced to a search for statistical significance (see Chapter 6 for more on this).

Statistical significance, then, is formally defined and involves testing that is repeatable (i.e. any two people could apply the same test to the same data and get the same result). Archaeological significance is much more difficult to pin down. Almost any identifiable pattern within a data-set can be subjectively analyzed and declared to be significant either because it is the same as some existing pattern or because it is different to some existing pattern, this involves testing that is often not repeatable.

While an increasing use and understanding of statistical techniques by archaeologists will not close this rift between the two different methodologies, it should provide alternative ways of approaching data.

Multivariate analysis (Chapter 12)
Some archaeological questions can be answered (and many more thought about) by using the relatively simple univariate and bivariate techniques described above. For many people and for many analyses these will be adequate. It has to be acknowledged,

however, that human beings and their resulting material and social worlds are multi-dimensional and complex. That complexity can not always be reduced to single variables or the relationship between two variables and this has resulted in a long history of applying multivariate statistical techniques in archaeology.

We would still suggest that, as for the simpler techniques, multivariates are used in an exploratory way. Many multivariate techniques produce some kind of graphical output (together with statistics) which is descriptive in the sense that it simplifies and presents patterns within the data. Chapter 12 offers a simple introduction to the two main areas of multivariate techniques that have been used in archaeology. The first is the general theme of clustering or grouping, the techniques of Principal Components and Factor Analysis, Correspondence Analysis and Cluster Analysis. Given several measurements on each of a set of objects can the objects be placed in groups so that within each group the objects are similar but between the groups there are interpretable differences. Secondly, given several measurements on a set of objects is it possible to predict a variable of interest from the others, and if so which variables are important in this prediction. These are the techniques of Multiple Regression and Discriminant Analysis.

Our argument for multivariate techniques being used in an exploratory way is a simple one. Because the statistics underlying these techniques are more complex than for descriptive and inferential techniques they are in more danger of being seen as a 'black box'. It is essential to use a computer and 'answers' are always provided whether or not you understand the manipulations being performed on the input data you have provided. In one sense the process is 'objective' in that the same result will always be attained from the same data whomever performs the analysis. In reality, however, it is a deeply 'subjective' process because firstly, we decide on which characteristics to measure and input as variables and, secondly, all of these techniques involve making decisions during the process. For example, there are several different methods of cluster analysis involving different ways of measuring the 'similarity' between objects and then displaying them. So, just as when using a histogram it can be enlightening to change the interval width and centre points, when using cluster analysis it can be interesting to experiment with different methods and settings.

CHAPTER 3

TABULAR AND PICTORIAL DISPLAY

3.1 Basic aims and rules.

Descriptive statistics involve the display and summary of data. Tables, diagrams and individual summary statistics enable a rapid understanding of the main characteristics of a raw data set. The parameters of individual variables, different relationships between two variables and trends and peaks within the data can all be recognised and quantified with these simple techniques.

This chapter describes tabular and pictorial descriptive statistics. The next two concentrate on the individual summary statistics usually classified as measures of central tendency and measures of dispersion. The techniques in all three chapters are exploratory in nature. They can be used together, several times over in different combinations, to draw out salient points from a data set.

For a table or picture to convey the maximum information, in a clear and unambiguous way, several simple rules should be followed:

1. Include a title.
2. All units of measurement must be clearly stated. If percentages are used try and include actual counts as well, or at least a total so that counts can be calculated.
3. State the source of the data if it is not obvious.
4. Use footnotes to define ambiguous or non-standard terms and to help clarification generally.
5. Use a key for all symbols and shadings.
6. Keep it simple so that the important information is not swamped by unnecessary detail.
7. Diagrams must be sufficiently large for any detail to be clear.

3.2 Tabulating measurements.

The starting point for any statistical analysis is a data set. This will consist of a table of observations which will be measurements at different levels as defined in Chapter 1. A table is made up of horizontal **rows** and vertical **columns** with a **cell** at each intersection which contains a value. Each row represents an item, sometimes called a case, and each column is an attribute of the item, usually called a variable. It is obvious that in Table 1.1 each row is one spearhead and each column is a variable as described in Chapter 1.

Table 1.1 shows typical archaeological data in the form of tabulated measurements. It consists of a mixture of categorical and continuous variables.

It is important that each row has a unique identifier. If this is not included within the list of variables (some kind of catalogue number, for example) then a new variable <ROW NUMBER> should be created. Each column should also be labelled with a <VARIABLE NAME>. Try to use meaningful variable names, even if abbreviated, rather than something like V1, V2, V3 etc.

The standardisation of units within a table can avoid confusion. This applies to all measurements for a single variable and to all variables within a table. All of the observations on the variable <MAXLE>, for example, are in centimetres. It would be unacceptable to have some recorded in centimetres and others in inches, or even in millimetres. All six variables in Table 1.1 that record a distance measurement are in centimetres. Again, it would be confusing if different units were used for different variables.

All six are also recorded to one decimal place with the decimal points aligned vertically. It is advisable to standardise the number of decimal places, certainly within the values of one variable and, if possible, within the whole table. This not only makes the table easier to understand visually but can also simplify future analysis.

3.3 Tabulating frequencies.
3.3.1 One variable.
It is usually the case in archaeology that a data set consists of a large number of items (rows). The tabulation of measurements, therefore, is of little use in trying to analyze the whole data set at any level. The usual way around this is to work with frequencies instead of measurements. A **frequency** (usually abbreviated to **f**) is the number of times a particular value (measurement) occurs, these are displayed in a **frequency table**.

If the variable is categorical, a convenient way of building up a frequency table is to use a system of **tally marks**. It can be seen from Table 3.1 that a tally mark is made for each measurement alongside the category into which it falls.

Condition	Tally	Frequency
1	//// ///	8
2	//// //// //// ///	18
3	//// ////	9
4	////	5
		Total 40 spearheads

Table 3.1. A univariate frequency table showing the condition of spearheads, <COND>.

The tally marks are bundled into fives using the 'five-bar gate' method. At the end of each row is a row total and at the bottom is a table total. In this example the variable is <COND>; it is ordinal with four categories. Because the table only describes one variable it is a **univariate frequency table**.

It is often of interest in archaeology to comment on proportions as well as counts hence it is common to convert the figures to percentages. Table 3.2 shows the same data as the last table but in a slightly different form.

Condition	Frequency	Percent	Cumulative Frequency	Cumulative Percent
Excellent	8	20.0	8	20.0
Good	18	45.0	26	65.0
Fair	9	22.5	35	87.5
Poor	5	12.5	40	100.0
Total	40	100.0		

Table 3.2. A univariate frequency table showing the condition of spearheads, <COND>.

Column one has category labels (sometimes called 'value labels') rather than the meaningless values 1, 2, 3 and 4. The second column shows category frequencies and the third shows category percentages. The fourth and fifth columns are **cumulative frequencies** and **percentages** established by adding consecutive category values. The cumulative figures can be of value if the table has many rows or if categories need to be combined. From the table above, for example, we could deduce that 65% (26) of the spearhead sample were in at least good condition and 35% (14) were less than good.

If the variable of interest is a continuous rather than a categorical variable a **grouped frequency table** should be used. This involves dividing the range of the values for the variable into classes and then proceeding as above (treating the variable as categorical).

There are no firm rules about how many classes to use although it is normal to have between five and fifteen of equal size. Less than five would lose too much information and more than fifteen would make the table too complicated. Classes of equal size give a better idea of the distribution of the variable, as shown in Table 3.3.

Interval (cm)	Frequency (f)
1.25 – 1.75	0
1.75 – 2.25	2
2.25 – 2.75	5
2.75 – 3.25	3
3.25 – 3.75	5
3.75 – 4.25	7
4.25 – 4.75	4
4.75 – 5.25	1
5.25 – 5.75	5
5.75 – 6.25	6
6.25 – 6.75	1
Total	**39**

Table 3.3. A grouped univariate frequency table for maximum width, <MAXWI>.

Table 3.3 shows the continuous variable <MAXWI> grouped into classes of 0.50 cm. It is important that class intervals do not overlap and have no gaps that could contain a value. With these data, recorded to one decimal place, an interval 1.3 to 1.7 would contain all true measurements from 1.250000..... to 1.749999..... This is replaced by the interval 1.25 to 1.75 as in Table 3.3. Although the value 1.75 occurs twice (in two different intervals) this will not cause a problem since the actual data value of 1.75 will never be recorded because of the accuracy of the data (it will be either 1.7 or 1.8). The precision of the class intervals will depend on the level of accuracy of the variable. If the coding is such that 'boundary values' do occur (values that could be assigned to two intervals) it must be decided whether to always put them into the lower or higher interval.

3.3.2 Two variables.

It is also possible to produce a frequency table for two variables at once. This is a **bivariate frequency table**, more usually called a **two-way contingency table**. Contingency tables are the basis of a group of statistical tests of significance which are described in Chapter 11. They are, however, also important in their own right as a means of rapidly assessing the relationship between two variables as shown in Table 3.4. Here, each spearhead has been assigned to one of the six cells according to its values on the two categorical variables <MAT> and <CON>. A tallying procedure similar to that described above is used to produce the six cell frequencies.

		Context			Group Total
		Stray find	Settlement	Burial	
Material	Bronze	19	1		20
	Iron	8	5	7	20
Group Total		27	6	7	40

Table 3.4. A bivariate frequency table (two-way contingency table), context, <CON>, by material, <MAT>.

If the variables are nominal or ordinal then the categories to be used will be their values (as in this case). If one or both of the variables are on a continuous scale then decisions about grouping the values will have to be taken. Sometimes the grouping of a variable will produce a contingency table with many empty cells (a sparse table). Such a sparse table can cause problems if statistical tests are to be performed so a common solution is to redefine the grouping to produce fewer groups with higher frequencies. This is discussed in more detail in Chapter 11.

Table 3.4 shows a 2 by 3 contingency table since it has 2 rows and 3 columns. The row and column sub-totals (20, 20, 27, 6 and 7) are called the **marginal frequencies** and the **table total** (40) is also shown. As with univariate frequency tables, proportions can be shown by converting the frequencies to percentages. Three different percentages can be calculated as shown in Table 3.5.

			Context			Group Total
			Stray find	Settlement	Burial	
Material	Bronze	Count	19	1		20
		Row %	70.4%	16.7%		50.0%
		Col %	95.0%	5.0%		100.0%
		Table %	47.5%	2.5%		50.0%
	Iron	Count	8	5	7	20
		Row %	29.6%	83.3%	100.0%	50.0%
		Col %	40.0%	25.0%	35.0%	100.0%
		Table %	20.0%	12.5%	17.5%	50.0%
Group Total		Count	27	6	7	40
		Row %	100.0%	100.0%	100.0%	100.0%
		Col %	67.5%	15.0%	17.5%	100.0%
		Table %	67.5%	15.0%	17.5%	100.0%

Table 3.5. A contingency table showing row, column and table percentages.

Each cell contains its frequency as a percentage of the row, the column and the whole table as indicated by the 'within cell order'. This shows the power of contingency tables in being able to present a lot of information quickly and simply. For example, Table 3.5 shows us amongst many other things that 67.5% of all our spearheads are stray finds, 70.4% of all stray finds are bronze and that 95% of all bronze spearheads are stray finds!

3.4 Pictorial displays for nominal and ordinal data.
3.4.1 The bar chart.
The bar chart is the most popular method of representing categorical data, it is sometimes called a 'bar diagram' or a 'block diagram'. The categories of the variable are positioned along the horizontal axis and a measure of popularity is the scale of the vertical axis.

A bar chart is a graphic version of a frequency table. The vertical scale can be in frequencies or percentages (in which case it is a **percentage bar chart**). If percentages are used the frequency for each bar should also be shown.

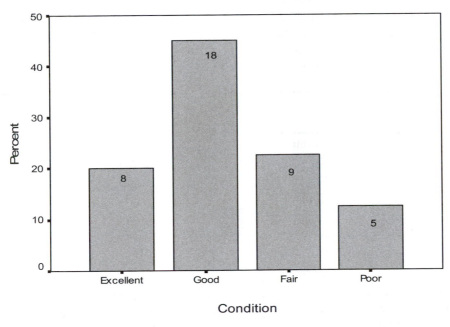

Figure 3.1. A vertical percentage bar chart for condition, <COND>.

The bars should be of the same width with each one separated by a gap to show that the variable is categorical and not continuous. It is quite acceptable to reverse the two axes and produce a **horizontal bar chart** with the bars horizontal. Figure 3.1 shows a vertical percentage bar chart with frequencies stated.

There are two variations of bar charts that allow the representation of two variables in one diagram. These are graphical equivalents to bivariate frequency tables. If we wanted to see how the condition of spearheads varied according to material we could use either a **multiple bar chart** or a **compound bar chart.**

Figure 3.2 shows a percentage multiple bar chart. Notice that the bars for the two categories of <MAT> are drawn together for each category of <COND>.

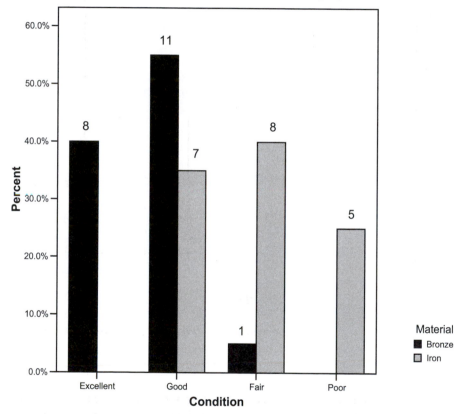

Figure 3.2. A vertical percentage multiple bar chart for condition, <COND> and material, <MAT>.

Figure 3.3 shows a compound bar chart. The bar for each category of <COND> is a total proportion (the same as Figure 3.1) divided according to the values of <MAT>. Both multiple and compound bar charts require some form of shading to represent the categories of the second variable together with an appropriate key.

20

If there are many categories (more than three or four) for the second variable, compound bar charts can become difficult to interpret and the multiple version may well be superior. Both Figures 3.2 and 3.3 are relatively simple and show the better reservation of bronze spearheads compared to iron.

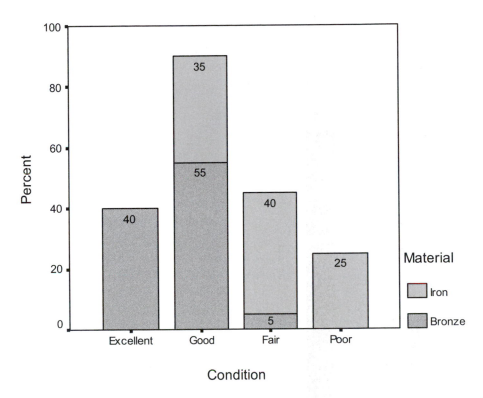

Figure 3.3. A vertical percentage compound bar chart for condition, <COND> and material, <MAT>.

3.4.2 The pie chart.
A pie chart is a circular diagram divided into sectors where each sector represents a value of a categorical variable. Each sector is proportional in size corresponding to the frequency (or percentage) value of that category. Figure 3.4a shows a percentage pie chart for the condition of the spearheads (equivalent to Figure 3.1).

Calculation:
When drawing a pie chart it is the angle at the centre which is proportional for each category. The proportion of 360 degrees can be calculated in the following way using the figures for Figure 3.4;

Excellent	= 20%	= (20/100) x (360)	= 72 degrees.
Good	= 45%	= (45/100) x (360)	= 162 degrees.
Fair	= 22.5%	= (22.5/100) x (360)	= 81 degrees.
Poor	= 12.5%	= (12.5/100) x (360)	= 45 degrees.

A protractor can then be used to draw the pie chart. If some of the sectors are so small in size that the labelling will not fit within them a system of shading and a key can be used.

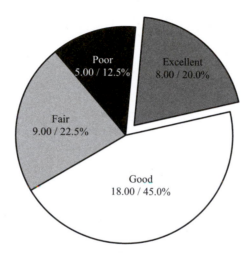

Figure 3.4. A pie chart showing proportion categories of condition, <COND>) exploded to emphasise 'excellent'.

If the purpose of the pie chart is to emphasise one particular sector this can be achieved by pulling out or 'exploding'. Figure 3.4 shows an **exploded pie chart** which focuses attention on the proportion of spearheads in excellent condition.

3.5 Pictorial displays for continuous data.
3.5.1 The histogram.
A histogram is the pictorial equivalent of the grouped frequency table; it displays a continuous variable that has been divided into classes. As with bar charts, histograms can be horizontal or vertical although the latter is much more usual (as in Figures 3.5 to 3.7).

There is a fundamental difference between a bar chart and a histogram. In a bar chart each block represents a category and block widths are equal so that frequency is measured by the height of each block. In a histogram the width of each block is proportional to the class interval (which need not be constant) and it is the area of each block that measures the frequency. It is usual to have equal class intervals but the choice of width can affect the appearance.

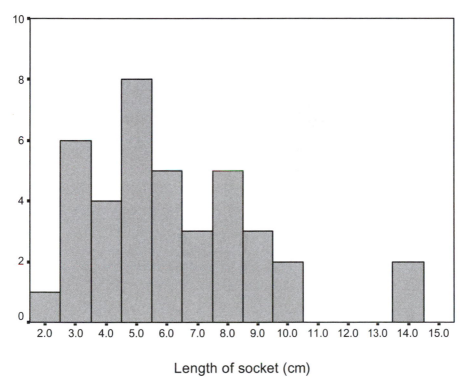

Length of socket (cm)

Figure 3.5. A histogram of socket length, <SOCLE>, with a 1cm interval.

Figure 3.5 shows a histogram of <SOCLE> with a 1.0 cm class width and class midpoints marked. Notice that adjacent blocks touch to indicate a continuous variable.

Notice also the relationship between the accuracy of measurement and class width. The interval 4.6 to 5.5, for example, is strictly from 4.55 to 5.55 since any socket length whose true value is 5.53 would have been recorded as 5.5 and a true value of 4.56 as 4.6. Because of this the class width is 1.0 exactly.

Figure 3.6 shows the same data as Figure 3.5 but with the class widths changed so that they are each of width 4 cm. Some of the details have been hidden but the overall shape is still clear.

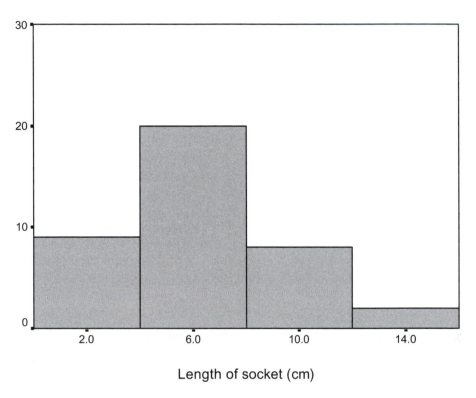

Length of socket (cm)

Figure 3.6. Figure 3.5 redrawn with different class intervals.

Because the values of the class width and the class midpoint for a histogram are under the control of the analyst, the use of histograms must be approached with caution. They are an exploratory tool which can produce many different results from the same data set simply by varying the class midpoint and/or the class width.

Figure 3.7 shows a histogram of <SOCLE> as in Figure 3.5 but with a class width of 3.0 cm instead of 1.0 cm and different midpoints as marked.

There are differences between Figures 3.5, 3.6 and 3.7 reinforcing the exploratory nature of histograms. It is probably a little naive and can certainly be misleading to produce just one histogram and accept it as the only interpretation of the data.

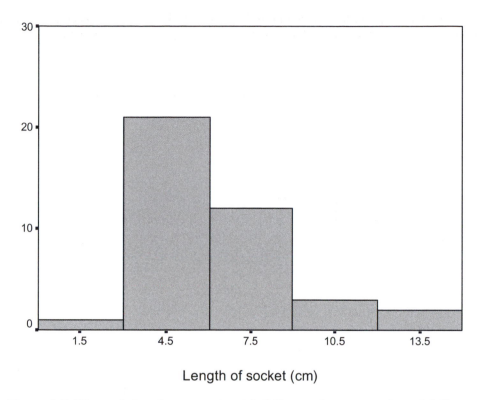

Figure 3.7. Figure 3.5 redrawn again with different class intervals and different midpoints.

3.5.2 The stem-and-leaf plot – an alternative histogram?
The stem-and-leaf plot (or stem-and-leaf display or stemplot) is a relatively new type of diagram which forms part of the approach known as Exploratory Data Analysis (EDA). It is similar in many ways to the histogram but has one important advantage. The stem-and-leaf plot displays the actual data values whereas a histogram displays only the frequencies of each class. Stem-and-leaf plots are designed for interval and ratio data.

Using the same data as Figure 3.5 (<SOCLE> which is column 9 in Table 1.1) we can see in Figure 3.8 how a stem-and-leaf plot is built up.

Each data value is split into two parts: a stem and a leaf, in this case the digits before the decimal point are the stem and those after the point are the leaf. The stem values are listed once only to the left of the vertical line and the leaves are added to their appropriate stems. Figure 3.8 shows the first ten values in column 9 of Table 1.1 plotted as stems and leaves.

stem	leaves
2	
3	11
4	56
5	28
6	61
7	8
8	
9	2
10	
11	
12	
13	
14	

Figure 3.8. The beginnings of a stem-and-leaf plot for socket length, <SOCLE>.

Figure 3.9 shows the diagram completed with all 39 values plotted. Notice that the leaf values have also been ordered within each stem to convey extra information.

stem	leaves
2	4
3	01114456
4	2355668
5	124589
6	0166
7	258
8	01467
9	26
10	2
11	
12	
13	5
14	4

Figure 3.9. The completed stem-and-leaf plot for socket length, <SOCLE>.

The advantage over histograms is immediately apparent because the original data values are recoverable from the stem-and-leaf plot. It can be seen that the distribution is biased towards the lower end of the scale, the distribution has gaps (stems without leaves) and that the two values of 13.5 and 14.4 are high outliers.

One decision to be made when constructing a stem-and-leaf plot is the size of the leaf unit. In Figures 3.8 and 3.9 the leaf unit is 0.1 and this indicates the units of the data values. Decimal points are not used in stem-and-leaf plots which means that the numbers 3500, 350, 35, 3.5 and 0.35 would all be split into a stem of 3 and a leaf of 5. The differences are indicated in the Leaf Unit statement as follows;

3,500	Leaf Unit = 100
350	Leaf Unit = 10
35	Leaf Unit = 1
3.5	Leaf Unit = 0.1
0.35	Leaf Unit = 0.01

The choice of leaf unit will depend on the particular application and on the range of values to be displayed. Complications can arise if a leaf contains more than two digits. The number 583, for example, may end up as a stem = 5 and a leaf = 8 with the three being dropped (leaf unit = 10).

Stem-and-leaf plots can become unwieldy with large data sets although it is possible to increase the number of horizontal lines per stem. For example, one stem value could have the leaf values 0 to 4 and 5 to 9 on a line each.

3.5.3 The ogive – the total so far.
The ogive (or cumulative frequency graph) is a graphical technique for showing cumulative frequencies as described in section 3.3.1. An ogive takes the form of a graph with the values on the horizontal axis representing the stated value **and all values below**. The vertical axis can be scaled in frequencies or percentages (or both). Ogives can be used for grouped data and for actual values of continuous data.

Figure 3.10 shows the same data as used in Figure 3.5, socket length, <SOCLE>, with frequencies as follows:

Interval (cm)	Frequency	Cumulative Frequency
1.55 – 2.55	1	1
2.55 – 3.55	6	7
3.55 – 4.55	4	11
4.55 – 5.55	8	19

27

5.55 – 6.55	5	24
6.55 – 7.55	3	27
7.55 – 8.55	5	32
8.55 – 9.55	3	35
9.55 – 10.55	2	37
10.55 – 11.55	0	37
11.55 – 12.55	0	37
12.55 – 13.55	0	37
13.55 – 14.55	2	39

For any value along the horizontal axis the corresponding point on the vertical axis shows how many are less than or equal to that value. In Figure 3.10, for example, 7 spearheads have a socket length of less than 3.55 cm and 37 less than 11.55 cm.

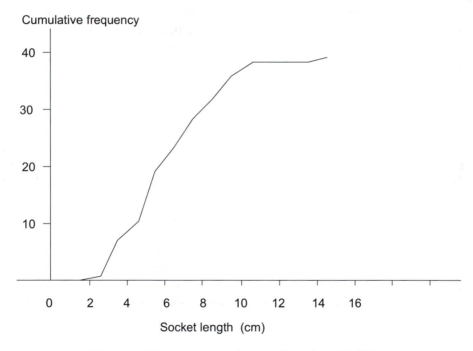

Figure 3.10. An ogive of socket length, <SOCLE>.

The shape of the curve betrays the nature of the distribution of the variable. The form of an ogive is that the curve is always increasing upwards. Large differences in consecutive class frequencies will produce a steep section of curve whereas small accumulations will result in a flat curve. It is convention to join the points of the curve on an ogive with straight lines.

The ogive allows the rapid assessment of some useful characteristics of a distribution. In Figure 3.10, for example, we can see that 50% of all the spearheads have a socket length between 2.0 and 5.0 cm and the other 50% between 5.0 and 14.0 cm. More formally, the Median, Quartiles and Percentiles of a distribution can be calculated from the ogive, these are described in Chapters 4 and 5.

3.5.4 The scatterplot – displaying two variables.

Most of the techniques described so far in this chapter refer to the display of a single variable, the exceptions are the bivariate frequency table and the multiple and compound bar charts. The scatterplot (or scattergram, scattergraph or scatter diagram) allows the plotting of the values of one variable against another variable.

Scatterplots provide a quick and easy visual estimate of the relationship (or correlation) between the two variables. It is essential that the two variables are **paired**; they must be two attributes of the same item or case. We can go further than this and state that they must be paired in an archaeologically meaningful way. For spearheads, the <MAXLE> and <AGE OF FINDER> (if available!) are paired variables which may be correlated although the relationship would be difficult to explain in archaeological terms, whilst <MAXLE> and <MAXWI> could well have a meaningful relationship.

Scatterplots can be drawn for variables measured at the ordinal, interval and ratio levels. A scatterplot takes the form of a graph where a horizontal (x) axis and a vertical (y) axis define an area of two-dimensional space. The axes are scaled according to the range of values for the variable each represents. It is standard practice for the points of lowest measurement to meet in the bottom left-hand corner. Each axis should be labelled with the variable name and unit of measurement.

As the two variables are paired the items will be positioned in the two dimensional space according to their values on the two axes. Points are marked with an appropriate symbol and not joined. Figure 3.11 shows a scatterplot of <MAXLE> and <MAXWI> from Table 1.1. This scatterplot shows a positive association or correlation between the width and length of spearheads suggesting that longer ones tend to be wider.

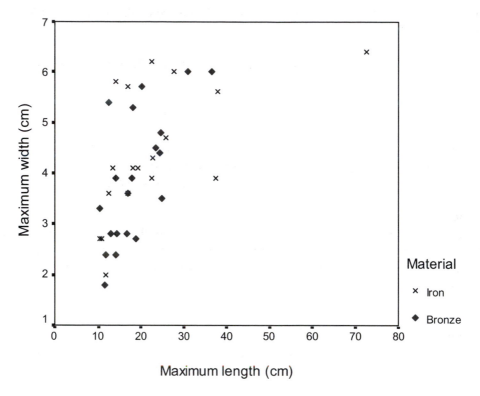

Figure 3.11. Scatterplot of maximum width, <MAXWI> and maximum length, <MAXLE> by material, <MAT>.

As in Figure 3.11, it is possible to introduce a third variable into a scatterplot. This must be categorical so that each category can be represented by a different symbol, in Figure 3.11 the two categories of <MAT> are shown. If too many different symbols are displayed on the same plot it can become confusing and difficult to interpret, three or four is the maximum. If two points fall on exactly the same position they are shown by a 2 on the diagram (or a 3 for three points etc.).

It is also possible to label each item on the plot for identification. In Figure 3.11 the unique value in column 1 of Table 1.1 could be displayed next to each point. Again, though, care must be taken not to overcrowd the diagram.

From a scatterplot it is possible to get a quick visual estimate of the correlation between the two variables displayed. This could be a positive or negative linear correlation, a non-linear correlation or a zero correlation. This visual estimate often forms the first stage of a more formal test of correlation and significance using one of the correlation coefficients that are available. These are explained in detail in Chapter 10.

Outliers such as the one large bronze spearhead in Figure 3.11 are immediately visible in a scatterplot.

The distributions could break down into different size groups which will often show as clusters of points in a scatterplot suggesting a classificatory line of enquiry. If we decided that the maximum width and the ratio of socket length to maximum length were significant enough variables to base a simple typology of spearheads on, a clustered result from a scatterplot would indicate classes or 'types'.

Points to remember:
Methods of tabular and pictorial display are some of the most important ways of presenting archaeological data and results, but only if they are capable of interpretation by the reader! Keep them simple, clear and uncluttered. Include information on the raw data where possible.

All of these methods are EXPLORATORY in nature. Use them in different ways on different variables to extract information from the data which could be of interest. It is often dangerous to just do one analysis and present the result as 'THE ANSWER'.

CHAPTER 4

MEASURES OF POSITION – THE AVERAGE

4.1 Introduction.

One of the less contentious uses of statistics is to condense and describe large bodies of data in a precise manner. Looking at the raw data in Table 1.1 it is impossible to get an immediate understanding of the spearheads because there is too much detail. What is an average spearhead? How many are larger or smaller than average? The tabular and pictorial displays of the last chapter go some way towards summarising and making sense of the data-set but it is possible to do more, and to be yet more precise.

Although the term 'average' is often used it is, in fact, very imprecise. When most people talk of the average (add up all the values and divide by the number of values) they are actually referring to the **mean**. There are two other common measures of position or average which are useful in archaeology: the **mode** and the **median**. It is important to use the correct term for the particular type of 'average' being used. All three measures have different advantages and disadvantages, the most suitable can depend on the level of measurement of the variable being used (see Chapter 1).

4.2 The Mode.

The mode is the only measure of position that can be used for nominal data. It can be used for variables measured at any level although interval and ratio variables are usually grouped.

The mode of a distribution is that value that occurs the most, i.e. it is the most popular, the most fashionable, it has the highest frequency.

Figure 4.1 shows a barchart of the ordinal variable <COND>, there are 8 spearheads in excellent condition, 18 are good, 9 fair and 5 poor. Value 2 (good) is the **modal class**, it is simply the most popular.

Figure 4.2 shows a histogram of the ratio variable <LOSOC>. The values have been grouped with a class interval of 0.1 cm.

Note that there are two classes with the highest frequency of 5, 1.65 to 1.75 and 2.35 to 2.45. This distribution is, therefore, **bimodal** and the two modes can be estimated to be 1.7 and 2.4. If there had been three modes it would be **trimodal**, etc.

Because the mode is a relatively simple statistic there are problems with it. It is an unstable measure and can swing wildly by the alteration of only a few values. Figure 4.3 shows a histogram of <DATE>: 300 to 400 BC is the modal class with a frequency

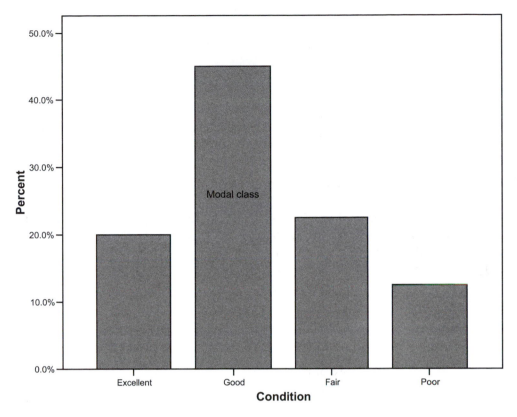

*Figure 4.1. The condition, <COND>, of the spearheads showing
the modal class.*

of 8. It would only take one more in the 800-900 group to make the mode very different. Also, the mode is not sensitive to frequencies in any of the other class intervals. They could all have values of 1 or they could all have values of 7, the mode would not alter.

It must be remembered when using a grouped interval or ratio variable that class intervals and midpoints can drastically influence the mode.

Despite these problems with the mode it is still often useful to know the 'typical' or 'most popular' value in a distribution. If the variable is nominal then there is no alternative, to speak of the 'average' is to use the mode.

The mode is also a useful measure if the distribution is asymmetrical (skewed) rather than symmetrical (see section 4.5).

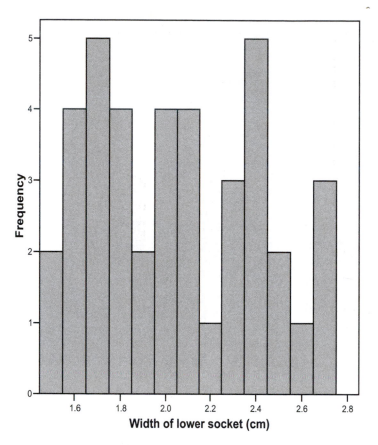

Figure 4.2. The bimodal distribution of socket width, <LOSOC>.

4.3 The median.

The median (from the Latin for 'middle') of a distribution is that value which cuts the distribution in half. One half of the values will be larger than the median and the other half smaller.

The median can be calculated for variables that are ordinal or higher but not for nominal variables. It is most suitable for ordinal variables.

Calculation:

List the values in order, for example the variable <DATE> as shown in Figure 4.3:

50, 100, 150, 200, 300, 300, 300, 350, 350, 350, 350, 350, 400, 400, 400, 450, 450, 450, 600, 600, 700, 700, 700, 800, 800, 800, 800, 800, 800, 800, 900, 900, 1000, 1000, 1000, 1200, 1200, 1200, 1200, 1200.

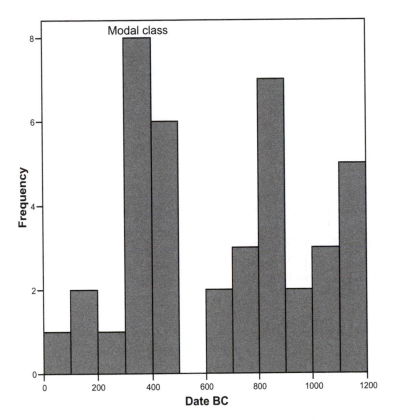

Figure 4.3. A histogram of date, <DATE>, showing the modal class.

If the number of values is even (40 in this case) the median (abbreviated to Md) is halfway between the middle two,

$$\text{Md} = \frac{20\text{th value} + 21\text{st value}}{2} = \frac{600 + 700}{2} = \frac{1300}{2} = 650$$

If the number of values is odd the median will be an actual value. Suppose the first spear in the list was not dated leaving only 39 values, the median is now the 20th value = 600. There are 19 values above and 19 below the 20th value.

Thirty-eight of the spearheads have a measurement for the variable <MAXLE>, the median is 17.8. It will be seen from Table 1.1 that although 17.8 is not an actual value there are 19 above and 19 below it.

The median can also be calculated from the ogive (see Chapter 3.5.3) by reading off the value of the variable (horizontal axis) that corresponds to half of the total frequency (vertical axis).

As with the mode, changes in just one or two values can have an effect on the median. In the <DATE> example above changing just the 20th value to 700 would cause the median to also change to 700.

The median, however, has the advantage of not being sensitive to occasional extreme values (**outliers**) which can seriously influence the mean (see below).

4.4 The mean.
Strictly speaking the mean described here is the **arithmetic mean**. There are other means such as the 'harmonic mean' and the 'geometric mean' but they are infrequently used in the social sciences and will not be detailed here.

The mean is the most common form of average and can be used on interval or ratio data but not nominal or ordinal.

The mean is the most important measure of position because a lot of further statistical analyses are based on it. Much standard statistical theory is devoted to testing means and the variation about the mean.

Calculation:
The usual notation for the mean of a variable x is $\bar{x}$ (x bar).
Sum the values and divide by the number of values.

Formula: $\bar{x} = \dfrac{\sum x}{n}$

where:

$\sum$ (sigma) = the sum of

x = the individual value

n = the total number of values.

Using the variable x = <MAXLE>:

$\bar{x} = 785.46/38 = 20.67$

Note that calculating a mean usually produces an answer to several decimal places, especially when using a calculator. Always round the answer down to a sensible level of accuracy when quoting it. In this instance the level of accuracy is meaningful but it may not always be so. Values that are recorded solely as integers could produce means to two or three decimal places – check that it is archaeologically sensible.

The mean is truly representative of a distribution if the values are grouped closely around a central value. It is sensitive to all values in the distribution, however, and can be very misleading. If the distribution is widely spread, unevenly distributed, has groups towards the extremes or even just occasional outliers, the mean on its own may not be a good measure of position or average.

4.5 Comparing the mode, median and mean.
It is important to understand that the mode, median and mean are three quite different measures of position which can give three different values when applied to the same data-set. The logic behind their calculation is different as they are measuring different qualities of the same distribution.

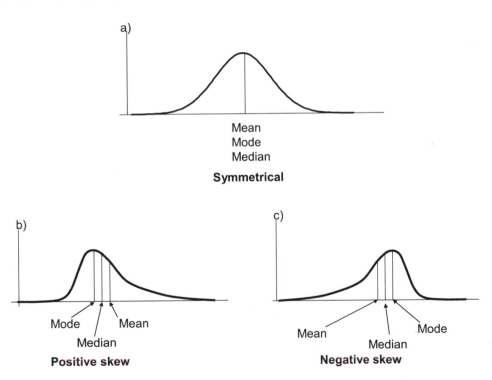

Figure 4.4. Symmetrical and asymmetrical distributions.

All three measurements are sensitive to the **symmetry** (or **skewness**) of the distribution. Figure 4.4 shows three hypothetical distributions, a) is symmetrical whereas both b) and c) are asymmetrical; b) is **positively skewed** and c) is **negatively skewed**.

All three measurements are read from the horizontal axis.

In the symmetrical distribution the mode, median and the mean all have the same value. Note that in both of the skewed distributions the three values are different with the mode at the 'highest' point, the mean towards the tail of the distribution and the median in between.

The mean can be affected by a few low scores in a negative skew or by a few high scores in a positive skew. In both cases it is not a good measure of position and if used alone would not accurately describe the distribution. For skewed distributions it is advisable to use all three measures as shown in Figures 4.5 and 4.6.

Width of lower socket

Class interval(cm)	f	cf
1.5-1.7	11	11
1.7-1.9	6	17
1.9-2.1	4	21
2.1-2.3	8	29
2.3-2.5	5	34
2.5-2.7	3	37
2.7-2.9	3	40

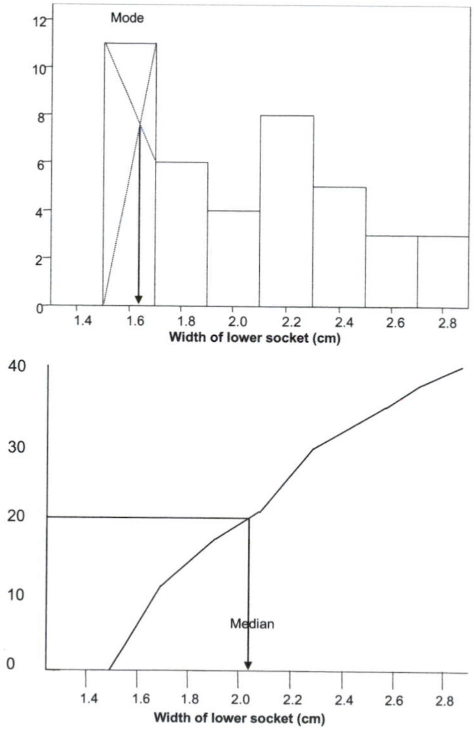

Figure 4.5. Frequency table, histogram and ogive for socket width, <LOSOC>.

Figure 4.5 shows the frequency table, histogram and ogive for the variable <LOSOC> with a class interval of 0.2 cm. (1.5-1.7 is really 1.5-1.699 etc.).

The distribution is fairly symmetrical with the following measures;

modal class = 1.5 to 1.7 (really 1.5-1.699)
mode = 1.64
median = 2.05
mean = 2.05

The modal class is 1.5 to 1.7 and the mode could be taken to be the middle of this interval. A more accurate estimate of the mode is obtained by using the simple 'cross' construction shown in Figures 4.5 and 4.6.

Maximum length

Class interval(cm)	f	cf
10-20	23	23
20-30	10	33
30-40	4	37
40-50	0	37
50-60	0	37
60-70	0	37
70-80	1	38

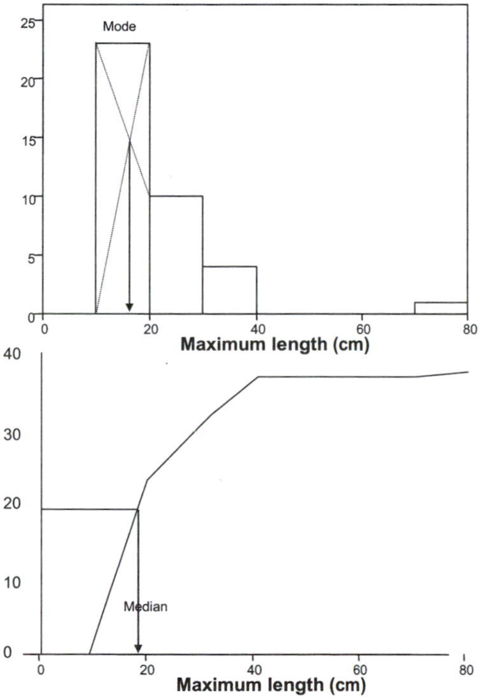

Figure 4.6. Frequency table, histogram and ogive for maximum length, <MAXLE>.

Notice that when <LOSOC> was discussed earlier (Figure 4.2) an interval of 0.1 cm was used and the distribution was bimodal. There are no absolutely definitively correct methods of describing data, different approaches may produce different results, which is why it is important to always state or define the techniques being used.

In contrast to Figure 4.5, Figure 4.6 shows a histogram of the <MAXLE> of the spearheads which is strongly positively skewed.

There is one very high value and several quite high values which are stretching the distribution in one direction to produce the following measures;

> modal class = 10-20 (really 10-19.999)
> mode = 16.0
> median = 17.8
> mean = 20.7

In these circumstances it could be misleading to quote just one measure as the 'average' length of the spearheads, all three together give a more accurate description.

Points to remember:
Be precise about which 'average' you are using. Depending on the level of measurement of the variable under investigation, try as many of the three methods as possible. Compare the results.

It is always useful to 'visualise' the data by using the simple graphical methods, as demonstrated here, rather than just looking at numbers.

CHAPTER 5

MEASURES OF VARIABILITY – THE SPREAD

5.1 Introduction.
Using methods described in Chapters 3 and 4 we can now display the distribution of a variable and give a measure of its central tendency in the form of a single value, its 'average' value. These alone are not enough to adequately describe a distribution as is shown in Figure 5.1:

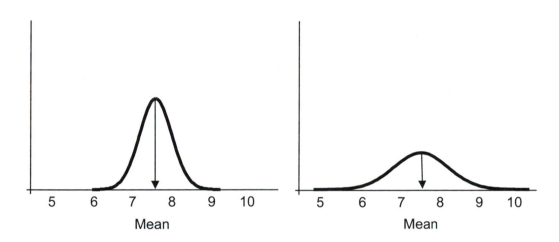

Figure 5.1. The spread of a distribution.

These two hypothetical distributions both have the same mean (and median and mode) but it is immediately obvious that they are very different. One has a wide spread of values while the other has values which are much more clustered around the mean. This chapter describes the main ways of quantifying the spread, or variation of a distribution, called **measures of dispersion** or **measures of variability**.

Measures of dispersion only apply to interval or ratio data.

5.2 The range.
The range measures the total spread of the distribution. It is a simple measure and is of limited use.

Calculation:
The range is calculated by subtracting the **minimum** value from the **maximum** value.

Example:
The variable <MAXLE> has a maximum value of 72.4, a minimum of 10.2 and a range of 62.2.

Because the range is such a simple measure there are problems with it. Like the mean, it is seriously affected by outliers (single extreme values). The <MAXLE> of the spearheads has an outlier with a value of 72.4 (look back to Figure 4.6). If this one value was removed the range now becomes $38.0 - 10.2 = 27.8$. The removal of this one value has altered the range from 62.2 to 27.8, a drop of 34.4 points.

The range can clearly only be used as a sensible measure of dispersion when all the values are clustered together. It gives the impression of an evenly spread distribution despite the presence of outliers.

5.3 The quartiles.
Another form of range, and one that eliminates the problems associated with outliers, is the **inter-quartile range** and its associated statistic the **quartile deviation.**

The **quartiles** are the three values in a distribution that partition it into four parts with an equal number of values in each part. They are usually referred to as Q_1, Q_2 and Q_3 so that 25% of the values are less than Q_1, 50% are less than Q_2 and 75% are less than Q_3, (Q_2 is also the median).

Using this same concept, the points that divide a distribution up into one hundred equal parts are called the **percentiles**. If a value falls on the 73rd percentile, for example, we know that 73% of the distribution is less than that value. During the discussion of probability and hypothesis testing in Chapters 6 and 7 the importance of the 5th and 95th percentiles will be shown. Occasionally **deciles** are used, with an obvious interpretation. The median, Q_2, 50th percentile and 5th decile are all different ways of describing the same value.

The inter-quartile range is the difference between Q_1 and Q_3 and the quartile deviation is half of this, ie. the deviation around the median.

Calculation:
The quartiles can be calculated in two ways:

1. Referring back to the method for calculating the median (Chapter 4.3), the data values are listed in increasing order and the list is then quartered. For the variable <DATE> this will produce the following quartiles:

$Q_1 = 350$
$Q_2 = 650$ (the median)
$Q_3 = 850$

Interquartile range $= 850 - 350 = 500$

$$\text{Quartile deviation} = \frac{850 - 350}{2} = 250$$

2. Draw an ogive (method as in Chapter 3.5.3). Draw horizontal lines from the 25%, 50% and 75% points on the vertical axis, when they hit the ogive line drop vertically and read off the values on the horizontal axis. Figure 5.2 shows the same ogive as in Figure 3.10 with quartiles calculated.

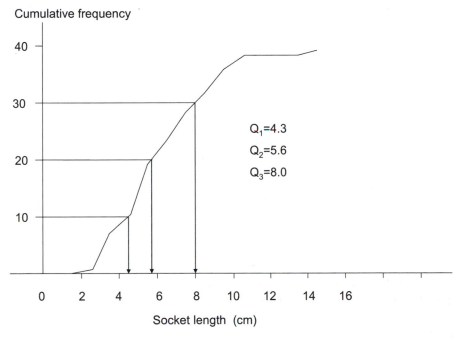

Figure 5.2. Calculating quartiles from an ogive for socket length, <SOCLE>.

The inter-quartile range is then found by subtracting Q_1 from Q_3. The quartile deviation is found by subtracting Q_1 from Q_3 and dividing by 2.

Formulae:

Inter-quartile range = $Q_3 - Q_1$

$$\text{Quartile deviation} = \frac{Q_3 - Q_1}{2}$$

The relationship between the quartiles and the range is summarised in Figure 5.3.

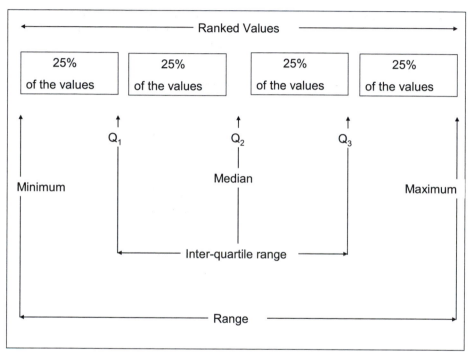

Figure 5.3. The quartiles and the range.

Example:

If we calculate the above for <MAXLE> of the spearheads categorised by the two values of <MAT> we get the following:

Bronze:

Min	Max	Range	Q_1	Q_3	Int-Quart Range	Quart Dev
10.2	36.6	26.4	13.12	24.17	11.05	5.53

Iron:

Min	Max	Range	Q_1	Q_3	Int-Quart Range	Quart Dev
10.2	72.4	62.2	13.07	26.25	13.18	6.59

The effects of the one large iron spearhead are obvious when the two values for the range are compared. The similarity between the two inter-quartile ranges, however, shows that there is not much difference between the variation in the maximum length of bronze and iron spearheads when all of the values are considered rather than just the two extremes. Figure 5.4 shows histograms of the two distributions with class intervals of 5 cm and class midpoints as marked.

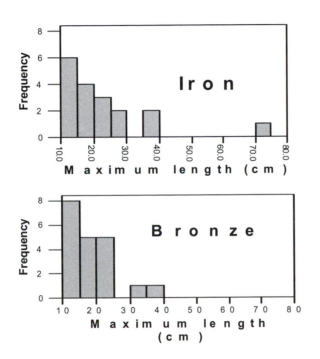

Figure 5.4. Distributions of the maximum length, <MAXLE>, by the two categories of material, <MAT>.

5.4 The mean deviation.
Another measure of dispersion is the mean deviation. This is also more reliable than the range because it is calculated using every value rather than just the two extremes. It also differs from the inter-quartile range and the quartile deviation because it uses every value rather than just the values at certain rank positions.

The mean deviation is a measure of how much each value deviates from the mean; it would, in fact, be more accurate to call it the mean of the deviations from the mean.

Calculation:
Calculate the difference between each value and the mean (ignoring the sign of the difference). Total the differences and divide by the number of values. This gives the mean of the differences which is the Mean Deviation.

Formula:

$$\text{Mean deviation} = \frac{\sum |x - \bar{x}|}{n}$$

where:

x = the individual value.

$| \ |$ = absolute value ie. ignore minus signs so that $|3| = |-3| = 3$

$\bar{x}$ = the mean of all the values.

$\sum$ = the sum of.

n = the number of values in the list.

Example:
For the two material categories of <MAXLE> of the spearheads the mean deviations are:

For Bronze:

11.4 – 18.68 = 7.28
16.6 – 18.68 = 2.08
10.2 – 18.68 = 8.48
18.6 – 18.68 = 0.08
24.4 – 18.68 = 5.72
Etc. for all 20 values

Total of differences
= 108.52

Mean deviation
= 108.52 / 20
= 5.43

For Iron:

12.4 – 22.89 = 10.49
22.6 – 22.89 = 0.29
17.9 – 22.89 = 4.99
16.8 – 22.89 = 6.09
13.3 – 22.89 = 9.59
Etc. for all 18 values

Total of differences
= 173.72

Mean deviation
= 173.72 / 18
= 9.65

Comparing these results with the range and the inter-quartile range above it is the most sensitive of the three if all the values are to be taken into account.

5.5 The standard deviation.
You may have realised that in calculating the Mean Deviation each deviation from the mean is treated as being positive even though half of them are negative! This is rather inelegant and is overcome in the calculation of the Standard Deviation by squaring each deviation from the mean. This also has the effect of weighting in favour of the larger deviations thus giving a more realistic measure of the dispersion.

The Standard Deviation is the most used measure of dispersion. It is important, as is the mean, because it forms the basis of further statistical tests. This also applies to the **variance** (the Standard Deviation squared) although this measure tends not to be used as a measure of dispersion because it can be a very large number.

Calculation:
The Standard Deviation can be abbreviated to: S.D., s, or σ (sigma, small s in Greek). Calculate the difference between each value and the mean. Square each difference. Total the squared differences to obtain the **sum of squares**. Divide the sum of squares by the number of values to obtain the variance. Square root the variance to find the Standard Deviation.

Formula:

$$S.D. \ (s) = \sqrt{\left(\frac{\sum (x - \bar{x})^2}{n} \right)}$$

The variance is usually called s^2 and has the following formula:

$$s^2 = \frac{\sum (x - \bar{x})^2}{n}$$

where:

x = the individual value.

$\sum$ = the sum of.

$\bar{x}$ = the mean of the values.

n = the number of values.

Example:
For Bronze <MAXLE>:

$(x - \bar{x})$	$(x - \bar{x})^2$
$18.68 - 11.4 = 7.28$	$= 52.998$ (7.28 squared)
$18.68 - 16.6 = 2.08$	$= 4.326$ (etc.)
$18.68 - 10.2 = 8.48$	$= 71.910$
$18.68 - 18.6 = 0.08$	$= 0.006$
$18.68 - 24.4 = 5.72$	$= 32.718$
Etc.	

Etc. for all 20 values

Total of the squared differences = 968.832

Variance = 968.832/20 = 48.442

S.D. $= \sqrt{48.442} = 6.96$

If this is applied to both of the material categories of <MAXLE> we get the following:

S.D. (Bronze) = 6.96
S.D. (Iron) = 14.85

Compared to the Mean Deviations calculated in the last section the Standard Deviations are quite different. The main difference is in the much greater value of the Standard Deviation for iron spearheads. This is because of the weighting that the Standard Deviation gives to values with larger deviations from the mean. The three large iron spearheads indicated in the histogram of Figure 5.4 are responsible for most of the variation in the maximum length of all iron spearheads.

It is worth remembering that the Standard Deviation never approaches anywhere near the range. As a rough rule of thumb when n=10 the Standard Deviation will be about one third of the range and when n=100 it will drop to about one fifth.

5.6 The coefficient of variation.
It is sometimes difficult to compare the spread of two or more distributions by just looking at the means and standard deviations. The actual values of these statistics could be of very different orders of magnitude. The coefficient of variation provides a comparative measure on a fixed scale from 0 to 1 (values remain positive) where:

towards 0 = a very narrow spread (small S.D.), and
towards 1 = very wide spread (large S.D.)

Calculation:
The coefficient of variation is usually denoted as V. It is found by dividing the Standard Deviation by the mean.

Formula:

$$V = \frac{S.D.}{\bar{x}}$$

Example:
The following table shows the means, standard deviations and coefficients of variation for the two variables <MAXLE> and <MAWIT> by material category:

	Maximum length <MAXLE>			Socket end to maximum width <MAWIT>		
	$\bar{x}$	S.D.	V	$\bar{x}$	S.D.	V
Bronze	18.68	6.96	0.37	8.63	2.82	0.33
Iron	22.89	14.85	0.65	9.87	4.34	0.44

One standard deviation of <MAXLE> for bronze spearheads is approximately one third of the mean (reflected in V= 0.37) whereas for iron spearheads the relative spread is greater at over one half (V= 0.65). The coefficient of variation, therefore, is a convenient way of expressing this comparison.

For iron spearheads the difference between the variability in the distance from the end of the socket to the maximum width and the variability in the maximum length is noticeable compared to the figures for bronze, (V= 0.44 and V= 0.65, V= 0.33 and V= 0.37). This suggests that iron spearheads have similar sized socket lengths regardless of their overall length, the half of the blade towards the tip is responsible for most of the variation in maximum length.

5.7 Standardisation.
Standardising values in a distribution is a similar concept to that just introduced with the coefficient of variation. It allows the comparison of values for different variables on a fixed scale. This is done by converting any value to a **z-value** (or **z-score**).

Consider a comparison between <MAXLE> and <MAWIT> for a bronze spearhead with a maximum length = 20.0 cm and socket end to maximum width = 13.0 cm. Comparing these values with the results given in the table above it can be seen that the

20.0 cm is a fairly typical length while 13.0 cm is an unusually high measurement. An objective way of measuring the 'typicality' of the two measurements is to convert them to z-scores. It is convenient to think of z-scores as units of Standard Deviation in relation to the position of the mean. A z-score of 1.0, therefore, is one S.D. away from the mean. For most distributions an interval of 3 SDs each side of the mean contains nearly all of the values, so z-scores usually fall within the range −3.0 to +3.0.

Formula:

$$\text{z-value} = \frac{x - \bar{x}}{\sigma}$$

where x is the raw or unstandardised value with mean $\bar{x}$ and standard deviation σ. Thus the standardised value for a maximum length of 20.0 is

$$z = \frac{20.00 - 18.68}{6.96} = 0.19$$

while for a socket end to maximum width of 13.0

$$z = \frac{13.00 - 8.63}{2.82} = 1.55$$

These results show that the value of 13.0 is 'relatively' larger or more extreme than the value of 20.0. The latter is very close to the mean of the distribution whereas the former, 13.0, is over one and a half S.D.s away from the mean of 8.63.

5.8 Boxplots.
Boxplots (sometimes called **Box-and-Whisker plots**) are a graphical representation of a distribution using some of the concepts described above. A boxplot divides a distribution according to the value of the inter-quartile range. Figure 5.5 illustrates a hypothetical boxplot with the appropriate terminology.

Calculation:
On an appropriate scale for the distribution the median is plotted as are Q_1 and Q_3. These are called the **lower hinge** and **upper hinge** respectively and the difference between them is the **h-spread**, they also form the **box**. 50% of the values are within the box. The whiskers run from each side of the box to the minimum and maximum values as defined below.

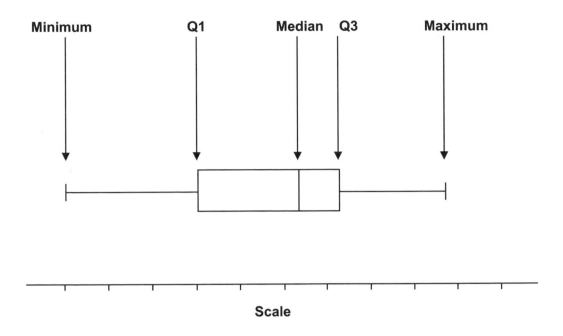

Scale

Figure 5.5. A boxplot.

At a distance of 1.5 x h-spread above and below the edges of the box are the **inner fences**. At a distance of 3 x h-spread either side of the edges of the box are the **outer fences**.

Any values that fall between the inner and outer fences are considered to be **possible outliers**, and any values that fall beyond the outer fences are **probable outliers**. The minimum and maximum points are found by ignoring any outliers of either type.

Example:
Figure 5.6 shows boxplots for the variable <MAXLE> categorised by material.

The boxplots show the larger spread of the iron spearheads (longer whiskers) despite the similarity in the size and position of the central parts of the two distributions (the median and the boxes which contain 50% of the values). The distribution of bronze spearheads is fairly symmetrical as shown by the central position of the median within the box. The assymmetry of the iron distribution is shown by the off-centre position of the median within the box. Remember that the S.D.s are 6.96 and 14.85 for bronze and iron respectively and the difference between these is reflected in the boxplots. Note that the iron distribution has one probable outlier at the higher end.

51

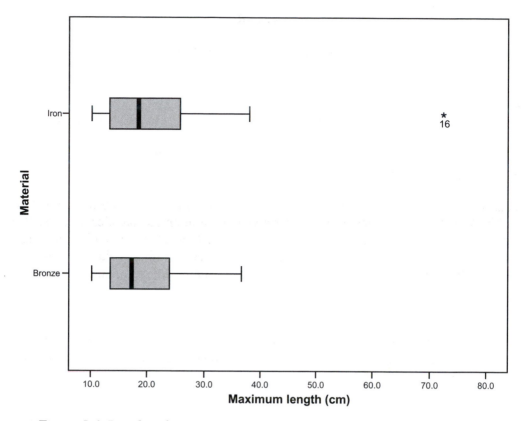

Figure 5.6. Boxplots for maximum length, <MAXLE> by material, <MAT>.

Without a proper investigation of the dispersion or variability of a distribution no meaningful comparisons or inferences can be made. Of all the different measures of variation the standard deviation is certainly the most used and together with its close relative the variance (SD = $\sqrt{\text{variance}}$) forms the basis for a great deal of statistical inference (see Section 2). We must repeat the emphasis on exploring the data – use different techniques and compare the results, use graphical representations whenever possible.

CHAPTER 6

AN INTRODUCTION TO PROBABILITY AND INFERENCE – DRAWING CONCLUSIONS

6.1 Introduction.

Section 1 was concerned with methods of descriptive statistics; describing, presenting and condensing data. These alone will often be enough to isolate trends and patterns within the data enabling certain archaeological questions to be answered and generating new questions to be asked.

This section goes one step further and introduces methods of formally testing patterns within data. These statistical tests are referred to as 'inferential statistics' because they are performed within a framework of hypothesis (or theory) testing and something is inferred from the result. In a nutshell, a certain pattern within the data is tested and found to be significant or not. Of course there are many different tests which can be applied and different levels of significance.

Important note: This chapter, together with the next, covers the three important areas of probability, inference and sampling. Both inference and sampling depend upon the concepts of probability and although sampling comes before inference in practice, here we discuss probability and inference together because of their close logical relationship.

At the heart of all inferential statistics are the concepts of randomness and probability. Many natural and artificial phenomena (including many archaeological data) are random in the sense that they are not predictable in advance although they do exhibit long term patterning. It is the study of these patterns (statistical distributions) which will involve probabilistic (also called stochastic or random) models.

The mathematical theory of probability was started by the two French mathematicians Blaise Pascal (1623–1662) and Pierre Fermat (1601–1665). Probability theory also owes a great deal to the work in 1933 of the modern day Russian A.N. Kolmogorov.

6.2 Probability – measuring chance and risk
6.2.1 The concept of probability

Three important definitions:

Definition 1. Often called 'a Priori' or Classical

For a complete set of n equally likely outcomes of which r are favourable, the probability of a favourable outcome is:

P(Favourable outcome) = r/n

Note the notation, P( ) simply means the probability of whatever is in the brackets, r and n are as defined above.

Definition 2. Often called 'a posteriori' or Frequentist.
For n past outcomes of which r were favourable, the probability of a favourable outcome is

P(Favourable outcome) = r/n

Both Definitions 1 and 2 will clearly produce a probability which is a measure within the range 0.0 to 1.0 inclusive. This is the standard way of stating a probability, so that:

a probability of 0.0 implies the event is impossible (eg. the probability of an iron spearhead being made in the Neolithic)

a probability of 1.0 implies the event is certain (eg. the probability of finding something important protruding from the baulk of an excavation on the last afternoon. JOKE!)

a probability of 0.3 implies the event has a reasonable chance of occurring but is not as likely as an event with a probability of 0.8.

Definition 3. Often called Subjective.
For a particular event, give a personal estimate of its probability using a scale of 0.0 to 1.0.

All three definitions have their place in archaeological analysis although Definition 2 is the most often used, assigning probabilities to past events. If a particular archaeological theory is to be tested (compared to the observed data) it is often necessary to use statistical theory based on Definition 1. In some cases, when investigating a new phenomenon or characteristic, Definition 3 is used to provide a first estimate of the probabilities.

Example 1
In the spear data-set of 40 cases (observations, trials or experiments using statistical language) there are 27 with a peg hole (see Table 1.1, variable number 5). Using Definition 2 with n = 39 (spearhead number 4 is not counted as it has missing values) and r = 27 we can conclude that the probability of a randomly chosen spear from among the 39 having a peg hole is:

P(peg hole) $= r / n$
                $= 27/39$
                $= 0.692$ (this is the same as 69.2%)

Note that probabilities are often stated as percentages. If a new source of spears is found and the assumption is that they are the same as the existing group, 69.2% of the new spears will have a peg hole. If this turns out not to be true the difference could yield interesting archaeological conclusions (testing such differences is discussed in Chapter 8).

Example 2
Of the 40 spears, only one has a socket length, <SOCLE>, less than 3cm, and so:

P(socl<3cm) $= 1 / 40$
                $= 0.025$

Any probability less than 0.05 (5%) is usually considered to be so low that, in this instance, it is improbable that a spear chosen at random would have a socket length of less than 3cm. Equally, any probability greater than 0.95 (95%) is usually considered to be very high (this introduces the concept of significance and is discussed below in section 6.4). It is highly probable, therefore, that a spear chosen at random will have a socket length of 3cm or more.

6.2.2 The concept of independence – are two events related?
For a spear chosen at random the probability that it is made of bronze and iron is clearly 0.0 since all of these spears are made of either bronze or iron but not both. The two events 'choose a bronze spear' and 'choose an iron spear' are said to be **Mutually Exclusive (M.E.)** – they cannot occur together. Other examples of such a dichotomy are Male/Female or Pig/Sheep etc.

A very important concept in probability theory, both generally and in archaeology, is that of independence. To illustrate this consider the classification of the 40 spearheads according to their material and whether or not they have a peg hole. We have already seen that

$$P(PH) = 27 / 39 \qquad\qquad\qquad P(\overline{PH}) = 12 / 39$$

where:
PH denotes does have a peg hole, and
$P(\overline{PH})$ denotes does not have a peg hole.

(Notice that $P(PH) + P(\overline{PH}) = 1.0$ as expected).

Since 20 out of the 40 are made of Iron and 20 out of the 40 are made of Bronze, we also have

$P(I) = 20 / 40$ $P(B) = 20 / 40$

If a spear has a peg hole, what is the probability that it is made of bronze? Does having a peg hole make it more likely or less likely to be made of bronze? If having a peg hole makes no difference to the probability of the material then the two variables (Peg Hole v Material) are **independent**, otherwise they are **dependent**. The following contingency table (see Chapter 3.3.2 for an introduction to contingency tables) illustrates these ideas:

Material	Peg Hole		
	Yes	No	
Iron	17	2	19
Bronze	10	10	20
	27	12	39

Using this table the following probabilities can be found:

P(Bronze and Peg hole)	= 10/39	= 0.256
P(Iron or Peg hole or both)	= 27 + 2/39	= 0.744
P(Iron and no Peg hole)	= 2/39	= 0.051

Returning to the earlier question, if a spear has a peg hole what is the probability that it is made of Bronze? The above shows that the proportion of all spearheads that have a peg hole and are made of bronze is 0.256 but the following calculates the proportion of those spearheads which have a peg hole which are made of bronze. Of the 27 spears that have a peg hole, 10 are bronze, so:

P(Bronze given it has a peg hole)	= 10/27	= 0.37
whilst:		
P(Bronze)	= 20/40	= 0.50

Since these two probabilities are not equal we can conclude that Material and Peg Hole are dependent. In fact, if a spearhead has a peg hole it is less likely to be made of bronze and so more likely to be of iron.

These ideas are often referred to as **conditional probability** and the example above would be written as:

P(B/PH)   = 0.37
P(B)   = 0.50

where:

B/PH   = bronze given it has a peg hole
B   = bronze.

Two important rules.

There are two simple rules which are fundamental to the understanding of manipulating probabilities:

Rule 1: If the two events A and B are mutually exclusive, then

$$P(A \text{ or } B) = P(A) + P(B)$$

ie. when using 'or' the probabilities are added.

Example. Since 8 spearheads are classified as Condition 1 and 18 as Condition 2 (Table 1.1, variable number 6),

P(C1)   = 8/40   = 0.20
P(C2)   = 18/40   = 0.45

and so:

P(C1 or C2)   = 8/40 + 18/40 = 26/40 = 0.65

Rule 2: If the two events A and B are independent, then

$$P(A \text{ and } B) = P(A) \text{ x } P(B)$$

ie. when using 'and' the probabilities are multiplied.

Example. If we assume that half of all spears are Bronze, then the probability of choosing two spears and both of them being bronze is,

P(1st B and 2nd B)   = P(B) × P(B)
                        = 0.5 × 0.5
                        = 0.25 (or 25%)

Note: To be strictly accurate this result should be (20/40) × (19/39) = 0.244 since having chosen one bronze spearhead from our forty there now remains only 39 of which 19 are bronze. These ideas are better illustrated with a second contingency table, this time showing the relationship between Condition and Material.

Material	Condition				
	1	2	3	4	
Iron	8	11	1	0	20
Bronze	0	7	8	5	20
	8	18	9	5	40

Since Condition 3 and Condition 4 are M.E., it is true that:

$$P(C3 \text{ or } C4) = P(C3) + P(C4)$$
$$= 9/40 + 5/40$$
$$= 14/40$$
$$= 0.35$$

However, Iron and Condition 2 are not M.E. since it is possible for an iron spearhead to be in good condition. From the table we have:

$$P(I \text{ or } C2 \text{ or Both}) = (8 + 11 + 1 + 0 + 7)/40$$
$$= 27/40$$
$$= 0.675$$

Compare this result with the incorrect (although easily done) way of doing it

$$P(I \text{ or } C2 \text{ or Both}) = P(I) + P(C2)$$
$$= 20/40 + 18/40$$
$$= 38/40$$
$$= 0.95 \text{ (WRONG!)}$$

This result is wrong because the score of 11 in the Iron/C2 cell of the table has been counted twice.

Notice that the table also yields:

$$P(I \text{ and } C2) = 11/40$$
$$= 0.275$$

whilst:

$$P(I) \times P(C2) \quad = 20/40 \times 18/40$$
$$= 0.5 \times 0.45$$
$$= 0.225$$

Since these two results are not the same, Rule 2 does not hold, Material and Condition are not independent. This means that the material of the spearhead does have an effect on its condition.

6.3 Probability distributions – predicting results

The data on spearhead condition, <COND>, can be transformed from a simple frequency count into a probability distribution by replacing each frequency with a probability, as shown below:

Condition	Frequency	Probability (or relative frequency)
1	8	0.200
2	18	0.450
3	9	0.005
4	5	0.125
Total	40	1.00

The variable <COND> is discrete (a condition of 2.3 is meaningless) and ordinal (condition 2 is better than condition 4). There are many different models (or theoretical distributions) which can be suggested as fits for the distributions of discrete random variables. The commonest two are the Binomial and Poisson distributions which provide good models for answering such questions as:

1. Of all graves in a cemetery, 23% contain beads. What is the probability that in a random sample of 12 graves more than five will contain beads? (Use the Binomial distribution).

2. The average number of sherds per sq.m. is three. What is the probability that in an area of 4 sq.m. there are less than five sherds? (Use the Poisson distribution).

Further discussion of these and other distributions are beyond the scope of this book, but see Chapter 13 for further reading.

For continuous random variables which are measured on a ratio, interval or ordinal scale (see Chapter 1.2 for levels of measurement) the most important model is the **Normal distribution**. It has many applications in archaeology and also plays a very important role in sampling theory. The normal distribution (recognised by the bell-shaped curve) is the most useful of all distributions because many naturally occurring distributions are very similar to it. Its mathematical derivation was first presented by De Moivre in 1733 but it is often referred to as the **Gaussian distribution** after Carl Gauss (1777–1855) who also derived its equation from a study of errors in repeated measures of the same quantity.

Consider Figure 6.1 which shows the distribution of the upper socket width, <UPSOC> for the 40 spearheads. The mean and standard deviation for this variable are 1.535cm and 0.331cm respectively (see Chapters 4.4 and 5.5 for calculating the mean and standard deviation). It can be seen that the widths vary more or less symmetrically about the mean with the more extreme values being less probable. This is typical of a sample from the normal distribution. Using statistical theory and tables (which are not relevant here) it is possible to produce a curve showing what an exact normal distribution with this mean and standard deviation would look like. This is shown as the smooth line in Figure 6.1. Figure 6.2 shows a normal distribution with a mean of 0 and a standard deviation of 1.

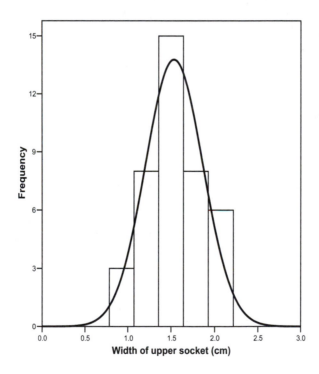

Figure 6.1. The distribution of the upper socket width, <UPSOC>.

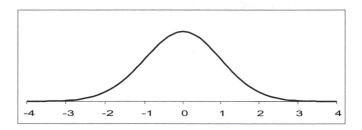

Figure 6.2. A normal distribution with mean 0 and standard deviation 1.

It can be shown that:

    (i) 50% of the values are less than 0
    (ii) 50% of the values are more than 0
    (iii) approximately 68% are between −1.0 and +1.0
    (iv) approximately 95% are between −2.0 and +2.0
    (v) exactly 95% are between −1.96 and +1.96
    (vi) exactly 90% are between −1.645 and +1.645
    (vii) exactly 99% are between −2.576 and +2.576

These results allow the following statements to be made for any variable with a normal or near normal distribution:

(a) approximately 95% of all values should be within two standard deviations of the mean
(b) practically all values should be within 3 SD of the mean

Example:
For the variable upper socket width, <UPSOC>, (Table 1.1, variable number 11)

Mean = 1.535, SD = 0.331

Therefore, we would expect about 95% of the values to be within $1.535 \pm 2(0.331)$ ie. within the limits (0.873, 2.197)

In fact there are two (5%) outside these limits with values of 0.8 and 2.2.

The variable maximum length, <MAXLE>, on the other hand, has a distribution which is clearly not symmetrical (Figure 6.3) and here the normal distribution is a poor model.

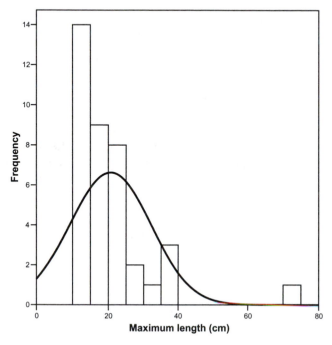

Figure 6.3. The asymmetric distribution of the maximum length, <MAXLE>.

The smooth curve shown in Figure 6.3 indicates the theoretical or expected shape of a normal distribution which has the same mean and standard deviation as those for <MAXLE>. If the underlying distribution of <MAXLE> really was normal, we would still expect small discrepancies between the expected and the actual (or observed) results from a sample, with such differences getting smaller for larger samples. In Figure 6.3 the differences between the observed frequencies and those expected from a normal distribution (or a model which assumes a normal distribution) are large, and so the normal distribution can be considered a poor model. There are formal ways of testing whether a normal distribution is a good model which are discussed in Chapter 9.

It is important here to mention the Central Limit Theorem (this is explained in detail in Chapter 7) because many statistical applications rely upon it. The Central Limit Theorem provides a rationale for the use of the Normal distribution which is why it is the most important of all distributional models.

6.4 The logic of hypothesis testing – is it significant?

Most of the rest of this section, and indeed most applications of inferential statistics in archaeology, are concerned with hypothesis testing (sometimes called tests of significance).

It is important to understand just what hypothesis testing in this formal context means. Theories of one kind or another abound in archaeology although many of them cannot be tested in any way let alone in the formal way to be described below. A hypothesis, therefore, must represent a quantifiable relationship and it is this relationship which is tested formally. We could say that all hypotheses are theories whereas not all theories are hypotheses.

In order to illustrate the logic of a hypothesis test consider testing the hypothesis that at least 40% of all bronze spearheads come from burials (this is the quantifiable association between the number of bronze spearheads and the variable <CON>).

The first step:
is to formulate two hypotheses, one is called the **null hypothesis** (denoted by H_0) and the other is the **alternative hypothesis** (H_1). This must be done so that one and only one **must** be true. In this case we would have:

> H_0: Proportion of bronze spearheads from burials is 40% or more
> H_1: Proportion of bronze spearheads from burials is less than 40%.

The second step:
is to take suitable measurements or observations from which a test statistic and its associated probability (described in step 3) can be calculated. Here we have a sample of twenty bronze spearheads seven of which have been found in burials (this is the observed result).

So far so good!

The third step:
is more difficult. Calculate a **test statistic** which can then be tested for significance in step 4. The test statistic allows for the calculation of the probability of the observed result which is often called the p-value. If H_0 is true and at least 40% of all bronze spearheads do come from burials what is the probability of a sample of 20 containing seven from burials? Using the ideas from Section 2.2 of this chapter we have:

P(Burial)	$= 0.40$ and so P(Not burial)	$= 0.60$
P(Not burial for 1st and 2nd)	$= (0.60)(0.60)$	$= (0.60)^2$
Hence P(Not burial for 13)	$= (0.60)^{13}$	$= 0.0013$

The p-value (probability of the observed result) is 0.0013 or 0.13% (very small!)

Step 4 (and last!):
Remember that the null hypothesis is being tested. The significance of the test statistic will determine whether the Null Hypothesis is accepted or rejected. There are set conventions for significance testing which allow this decision to be made.

The p-value calculated above is very small which means either H_0 is true and we have been very unlucky in drawing an unrepresentative sample, or else H_0 is false. The convention for significance testing is as follows:

If $p<0.05$ (5%) reject H_0 at the 5% level and conclude that there is significant evidence to show that the percentage of bronze spearheads from burials is less than 40% (in other words if H_0 is rejected H_1 **must** be accepted). It is also valid to conclude that we are 95% certain that the percentage of bronze spearheads from burials is less than 40%.

If the p-value had turned out to be greater than 0.05, the conclusion would have been that there is insufficient evidence to reject H_0 at the 5% level and so H_0 is accepted. A somewhat philosophical point here – it is impossible to **prove** a hypothesis in this formal way, it is either accepted or rejected at certain levels of significance. In a way this is in line with the falsificationist views of Karl Popper and has interesting implications for archaeology by suggesting that the advancement of knowledge is not based on proving things but on disproving things. If, for example, we reconstruct an Iron Age roundhouse and it falls down the first time the wind blows, it is reasonable to argue that this disproves that building hypothesis. If, however, it stands for many years it doesn't prove that that is how roundhouses were built in the Iron Age. Which advances knowledge more?

Although the 5% significance level has been used above other levels can also be applied, those often used in the social sciences are:

> $p<0.10$ reject at the 10% level
> $p<0.05$ reject at the 5% level
> $p<0.01$ reject at the 1% level
> $p<0.001$ reject at the 0.1% level.

Important note:
having said this about significance levels it is important to emphasise the arbitrary nature of the whole concept of significance (we thank Clive Orton for forcing this issue). We have explained the statistical reasoning behind significance levels but it is up to the archaeologist to justify the choice of a certain significance level in

archaeological terms. Is the decision to accept or reject the null hypothesis important enough to warrant a 1% level or will 5% do, or why not 7%? What are the archaeological costs involved in accepting or rejecting the null hypothesis? If lives depended on the outcome, as in testing drugs or parts of aircraft, we could easily justify using the 0.1% level but the situation is not so clear cut in archaeology.

Returning to the p-value of 0.0013 we can now see that H_0 can be rejected at the 1% level concluding that we are **at least** 99% certain (this is not absolutely true but will do in simple terms) that the percentage of spearheads from burials is less than 40% (to be precise we are 99.87% certain but it is convention to stick to the 10%, 5%, 1% and 0.1% levels).

In the four steps described above it is the calculation of the test statistic and its associated probability that can be difficult. In various situations and under various assumptions there are a number of accepted methods of doing this, Chapters 8 to 11 describe some of them

CHAPTER 7

SAMPLING THEORY AND SAMPLE DESIGN

7.1 Introduction.

Archaeologists are permanently working with samples. An area of excavation is a sample of the complete site which in itself is a sample of all sites of that type. The same goes for artefact assemblages which represent samples of a larger, often unknown, group. For many years such samples have been selected by a variety of *ad hoc* methods and have served archaeology well, indeed, virtually all of our current archaeological knowledge rests upon the results from thousands of judgement samples, so called because they are chosen in a mathematically non-rigorous manner.

This chapter is about a different type of sampling, usually called **random sampling** in the UK or **probability sampling** in North America because it uses ideas from probability theory. Strictly speaking, judgement samples do not allow any statements to be made about the material that was not included in the sample (although archaeologists do this all the time) whereas random sampling provides a means of making such statements within a stated confidence limit. If a 20% sample of the interior of a hillfort was excavated, and the sample was a random one, it would be possible to estimate the number of sherds, pits or any other characteristic for the whole interior within stated confidence limits. If the sample was a judgement sample, as most excavations are, any statements made concerning the whole would be informed guesswork.

The essence of all sampling is to gain the maximum amount of information by measuring or testing just a part of the available material. Because of the ability of random sampling to enable extrapolation from the sample taken it can often provide more information than a judgement sample although, of course, the procedure of random sampling is more difficult to set up and perform. Before going any further, some formal definitions need to be established:

Population: the whole group or set of objects (or other items) about which inference is to be made. This could be all Bronze Age spearheads or all spearheads in some sub-set (e.g. a particular county).

Sampling frame: a list of the items, units or objects that could be sampled. Often, and ideally, the sampling frame will contain all of the population, but it need not.

Variable: a characteristic which is to be measured for the units, such as weight of spearheads.

Sample: the subset or part of the population that is selected.

Sample size (n): the number in the sample. A sample size of 5 is considered small, while, formally, a sample size of 50 is large. The sample size may be stated as a percentage of the sampling frame, e.g. a 10% sample.

Clearly, the larger the sample size, the more reliable will be any inferences made from the sample (and, usually, the more costly in time and resources it will be to collect). A smaller sample will be less expensive although the resulting information will be less reliable. Faced with a cemetery of 127 graves, excavating a sample of 100 should allow reliable inferences about the whole group, whereas inferences from a sample of only 10 would be very unreliable. As with judgement sampling, the size of the sample is often a product of many constraining factors.

The rest of this chapter is concerned with two important aspects of sampling:

(i) How to make the sample as representative of the population as possible so that it yields the maximum information.

(ii) Having taken a sample, how to measure the precision or reliability of the results it produces.

7.2 Sampling strategies – which measurements to take.
The following are the more common and useful sampling strategies for drawing a random sample. It should be emphasised, however, that it is often difficult to apply these rigidly in many archaeological situations. They are not claimed to be a substitute for archaeological intuition and experience, but a useful tool to be used when and where appropriate.

Each method will be applied to designing a sample of 10 spearheads from our population of 40 (a 25% sample) in order to estimate the mean weight. We know that the mean weight of all 40 is 442.4 g and the S.D. = 436.0 g.

A Simple random sample.
Each unit in the population has the same chance of being selected as any other unit. To take a simple random sample of 10 spearheads we could:

(a) Stick a pin into the list ten times without looking (not professional and open to abuse, fiddling and criticism!)

(b) Put the 40 spearheads into a large box, shake and withdraw 10 (not a good idea, think of at least three faults!)

(c) Number the spearheads 1 to 40 and using random number tables identify 10 by choosing numbers from the tables. This is the usual method which is sometimes improved upon by using a computer to select the random numbers. Table A in the Appendix is a typical table of random digits between 0 and 9. They are grouped into blocks of 5 just for ease of reading. If we were to start reading at the top left and read across (we could start reading anywhere but should then read from the table in a steady sequence either down, up or across), the first number would be 72, the second 31, then 02, 85, 27 etc. This will give a sample of 10 spears to be numbers:

31, 2, 27, 33, 8, 26, 23, 29, 22, 21.

Notice that 00 and any number larger than 40 has been ignored, and if we had the same number twice this would also have been ignored. Using this 10% sample the mean weight is 349.51 g which is rather low compared to the true mean of 442.4 g.

A Systematic sample.
To take a systematic sample of 10 from our population of 40 spearheads take every fourth one. Although in this example we start with number one, strictly speaking the start number (between one and four) should be chosen at random. This method has the advantage of being easy to design although if the units have inherent patterning in their ordering systematic sampling could be inappropriate. Our sample starts at number one and ends with number 37 (numbers 1, 5, 9, 13, 17, 21, 25, 29, 33 and 37) producing a sample mean weight of 405.68 g (true mean is 442.4 g).

A Stratified sample.
In order to get a representative sample the structure of that sample should reflect the structure of the population in terms of characteristics that are thought to be influential. For example, the spearhead population consists of 20 iron and 20 bronze items which could influence the weight (if one group was a lot heavier than the other), in order to reflect this our sample should contain 5 iron and 5 bronze spearheads. Using the random number tables again (Table A in the Appendix), we select numbers in the range 1 to 40 in order to give the first 5 iron and 5 bronze:

Iron: 2,   8,   13, 17, 4
Bronze: 31,   27, 33,   26, 23,

These give a sample mean of 409.43; still a little low. Perhaps there is no real relationship or association between material and weight, in which case stratifying using material as a stratum has no advantage, (to test this claim see the measures of association for categorical data described in Chapter 11).

If the context the spearhead was found in is suspected to have a relationship to weight, then we should stratify our sample using context as a stratum. The 40 spearheads are spread between the three contexts as follows:

Context	1	2	3
Number of spearheads	27	6	7
Percentage of total	67.5%	15.0%	17.5%

This means that to design a sample of 10 that is stratified proportionally according to context, we would need to take 67.5% of the 10 from context 1 etc. Using nearest whole numbers (in order to save having to saw spearheads into bits!) the 10% sample would consist of the following:

context 1	context 2	context 3
67.5%	15%	17.5%
7 spearheads	1 spearhead	2 spearheads

Again using the random number table and only taking numbers between 1 and 40, the following proportional stratified random sample is taken (starting top left in the table and going down in pairs):

Context 1: 38, 14, 26, 31, 40, 13, 34
Context 2: 8
Context 3: 7, 4

The mean weight of this sample is 398.6 g, again a little low. By designing such a stratified sample there is no guarantee that the results will be more accurate or better but we are less likely to produce unrepresentative results based on some bias in the sample.

A Cluster sample.
Rather than select individual items, select clusters or groups of items that are close together. This would be better illustrated by a spatial application where, for example, a survey of a large area is being conducted. To save on travelling time, groups of sites are selected at random, if each group is then sampled individually this could be called a two stage sampling design.

A Convenience Sample.
This sampling design does not use random methods to select the sample, and consequently can produce poor results. If, for example, the first 10 spearheads were taken as the sample (simple because this is convenient) the mean would be 304.99 g which is very low. If the next 10 are taken their mean is 664.94 g which is very high.

There are other sampling strategies, although the first three described above are the main ones and certainly adequate for most archaeological applications.

7.3 A statistical background to sampling.
Once a sample has been taken various statistics can be calculated from it (using methods described in Section 1 of the book). The commonest of these sample statistics are:

$\bar{x}$, the sample mean
s, the sample standard deviation, and
p, the sample proportion, i.e. the proportion of the sample having a particular characteristic.

The true or population values for these statistics are usually unknown, and formally denoted by Greek letters so that:

$\bar{x}$, the sample mean, is an estimate of μ, the population mean
s, the sample standard deviation, is an estimate of σ, the population standard deviation
p, the sample proportion, is an estimate of π, the population proportion.

7.3.1 The central-limit theorem – the law of averages.
In order to comment on how good an estimate the sample statistics are, the nature of their distribution needs to be known. To illustrate this, consider trying to estimate the mean weight of the spearheads from a sample of only 9 randomly chosen ones. We know that for the population of 40, $\mu = 442.4$ and $\sigma = 436.0$. Figure 7.1 shows the distribution of weight for the whole population which is not symmetrical (it is skewed) with a large amount of variation ($\sigma = 436.0$).

If a simple random sample of 9 spearheads is taken, and the sample mean calculated, we would expect it to be a reasonable estimate of the truth (the population mean). If many such random samples are taken each will produce an estimate of the population mean and we would expect most of them to be near to the truth. Figure 7.2 shows the distribution of 40 sample means each one calculated from a separate random sample of

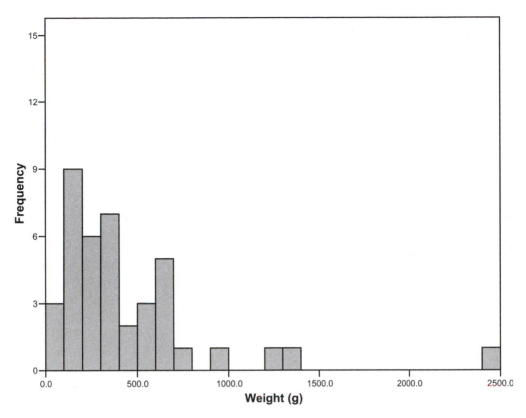

Figure 7.1. The distribution of weight, <WEIGHT>.

9 spearheads. (We have taken a sample size of 9 for reasons that will become clear later, but these ideas hold whatever the sample size).

Comparing the two distributions shown in Figures 7.1 and 7.2, original weights and sample mean weights, the differences in shape can be seen. This demonstrates two important concepts of sampling which together form the Central Limit Theorem, (here this theorem is only demonstrated then stated but it can be proved formally),

(i) The distribution of the sample means is reasonably symmetrical and can be well modelled by the normal distribution (see Chapter 6 for the importance of this). As the sample size increases so the closeness of the approximation to the normal distribution increases. For most distributions a sample size as low as four will produce a fair approximation, while a sample of 20 or 30 will give a very good approximation, (this is why a sample of 50 is considered to be large). The sequence in Figure 7.3 (a to e) shows how the distribution of sample means becomes more symmetrical as the sample size increases.

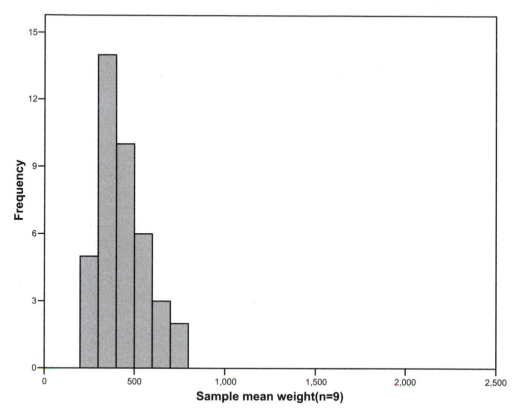

Figure 7.2. The distribution of mean weight, <WEIGHT> for samples of size nine.

(ii) These distributions also show that the variation is reducing as the sample size increases. Variation is usually measured by the standard deviation and the following table shows how the SD changes as the sample size increases from 1 to 25 individuals:

Sample size (n)	Standard Deviation
1	436.0
4	182.6
9	129.7
16	75.9
25	54.1

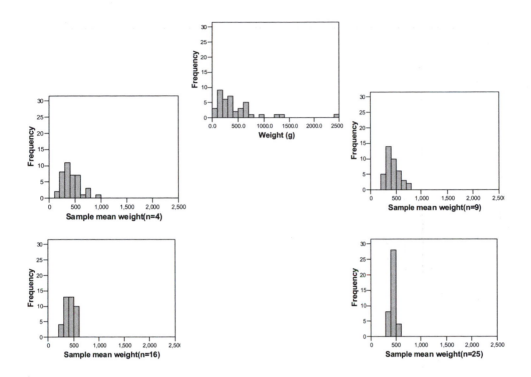

Figure 7.3. The change in the distribution of sample means as sample size increases.

It can be proved that if the standard deviation of the individuals in a population is σ, then the standard deviation of the means of samples of size n, often called the **standard error**, of the mean (or simply the SE of the mean) is

$$SE \text{ (mean)} = \frac{\sigma}{\sqrt{n}}$$

The results in the table above confirm this since by taking samples of size 4, the original SD has been approximately halved and for n = 9 the SD is reduced to approximately one third.

Before discussing the implications of this any further, the Central Limit Theorem can be stated (without proof);

If a random sample of size n is taken from a population with mean μ and SD σ, then:

(1) the sample means are approximately normally distributed with this approximation becoming closer as n increases,

(2) the mean of the sampling distribution is μ

(3) the SD of the sampling distribution is $\dfrac{\sigma}{\sqrt{n}}$

The important consequence of this theorem is that whenever a population mean is to be estimated we are able to use the known characteristics of the normal distribution (see Chapter 6) to evaluate how precise or reliable our estimate is. For example, if we had been trying to estimate the population mean for weight from a sample of just 9 spearheads, by looking at Figure 7.3(c) we can see that the truth is between approximately 300 g and 700 g. If we had a larger sample of 25 we could estimate the true mean to be between 400 and 500 g (Figure 7.3 (e)).

7.3.2 Confidence limits – the reliability of results.
Although the estimates for the true mean get more accurate as the sample size increases they are still rather vague. It is statistical convention to calculate a **confidence interval** (or **confidence limits**) for an estimate based on a particular probability value, usually 90%, 95% or 99%. This is a formal way of stating confidence in the estimate. Given a sample of n observations which lead to a sample mean of $\bar{x}$, from a population with unknown mean but standard deviation σ, confidence limits are calculated as below.

In practice, when trying to estimate the mean, the standard deviation is also unknown but for large samples the calculated standard deviation is often taken to be the actual true standard deviation. When the sample size is small so that the sample standard deviation is a poor estimate for the true standard deviation, the following theory should be modified by using the Students-t distribution to calculate the confidence limits. Confidence intervals are calculated using:

Confidence level	Confidence intervals
90%	$\bar{x} \pm 1.645 \dfrac{\sigma}{\sqrt{n}}$
95%	$\bar{x} \pm 1.960 \dfrac{\sigma}{\sqrt{n}}$

99% $\qquad\qquad\qquad\qquad\qquad\qquad \bar{x} \pm 2.576\dfrac{\sigma}{\sqrt{n}}$

If we had taken a sample of 16 spearheads and calculated $\bar{x}$ = 402.1, then using σ = 436.0 would give 95% confidence limits of:

$$402.1 \pm 1.969 \dfrac{436.0}{\sqrt{16}}$$

$$= 402.1 \pm 1.960(109.0)$$
$$= 402.1 \pm 213.64$$

i.e. from 402.1 − 213.64 to 402.1 + 213.64
from 188.46 to 615.74

We could conclude from this that it is 95% certain that the true mean is between 188.46 g and 615.74 g. If these limits are too wide, as they probably are, then clearly a larger sample needs to be taken to reduce them (the importance of $\sqrt{n}$ in the equation). In fact these very broad limits reflect the high variability (standard deviation) in the weight of the spearheads. If we consider our 40 spearheads as a sample of some larger population (all spearheads perhaps), then we can calculate the 95% Confidence Limit for the mean weight to be:

$$442.4 \pm 1.96 \dfrac{436.0}{\sqrt{40}}$$

$$= 442.4 \pm 135.1$$

i.e. we are 95% sure that the mean weight of all spearheads is between 307.3 g and 577.5 g. This is still rather a poor estimate because of the large standard deviation which we can see is mainly due to one spearhead having an unusually high weight (number 16 in Table 1.1, at 2446.5 g). We could, of course, omit this one spearhead from our calculations considering it to be an unrepresentative outlier or freak. This would produce a better (narrower) confidence interval but such editing of the data is archaeologically dangerous without sound justification.

If, instead of estimating the population mean, we were interested in estimating the proportion of the population with a particular characteristic, then similar ideas are used to establish confidence limits for this proportion. If a sample of size n gives a proportion of size p, then the various confidence limits are given by:

Confidence level	Confidence limits
90%	$p \pm 1.645 \sqrt{\dfrac{p(1-p)}{n}}$
95%	$p \pm 1.960 \sqrt{\dfrac{p(1-p)}{n}}$
99%	$p \pm 2.576 \sqrt{\dfrac{p(1-p)}{n}}$

Consider that our 40 spearheads are a sample from a much larger unknown population, and we need to estimate the true proportion of bronze spearheads that have loops. Of the 20 bronze spearheads in our sample, 9 have loops giving a sample proportion of 9 in 20, = 9/20 = 0.45 or 45%.

If we wanted to compare this proportion to another population (perhaps another site, area or assemblage) we need to know just how reliable this figure of 45% is. Given that n = 20 and p = 0.45, the 95% confidence limits for the true proportion are:

$$0.45 \pm 1.96 \sqrt{\frac{0.45(1-0.45)}{20}}$$

$$= 0.45 \pm 1.96 \sqrt{0.012375}$$

$$= 0.45 \pm 0.218$$

i.e. from 0.232 to 0.668

This means that with a sample of 20 we can be 95% certain that the true proportion of bronze spearheads is somewhere between 0.232 and 0.668 (23% and 67%). Again this is rather vague, but this in itself serves to emphasise the need to quote confidence limits – to show the uncertainty.

The previous formulae for confidence limits can also be used to estimate the required sample size to obtain a given level of reliability. Suppose that we really wanted to estimate the true proportion of bronze spearheads with loops to within $\pm 0.05 \, (\pm 5\%)$ i.e. with 95% certainty. Given that $p = 0.45$, what sample size is needed?

The 95% confidence limits are:

$$0.45 \pm 1.96 \frac{\sqrt{(0.45)(1-0.45)}}{\sqrt{n}}$$

i.e. $\quad 0.45 \pm 1.96 \frac{\sqrt{(0.45)(0.55)}}{\sqrt{n}}$

We need to substitute the 'error' part of the above with the required level of ± 0.05, so:

$$0.05 = \frac{1.96\sqrt{(0.45)(0.55)}}{\sqrt{n}}$$

i.e. $\quad \sqrt{n} = \frac{1.96\sqrt{(0.45)(0.55)}}{0.05}$

$$\sqrt{n} = 19.5$$

$$n = 19.5^2$$

$$n = 380.3$$

Hence we need a sample of 380 bronze spearheads to give an estimate of the proportion with loops with a confidence level of 95%. To save doing the previous analysis there are simpler formulae to find the required sample size, n, to estimate either the mean or proportion to within $\pm D$ (here with 95% confidence):

$$\text{Mean: } n = \left[\frac{1.96\sigma}{D} \right]^2$$

Proportion: $n = \left[\dfrac{1.96\sigma}{D}\right]^2 p(1-p)$

So, for the previous example where $D = 0.05$ and $p = 0.45$

$$n = \left[\dfrac{1.96}{0.05}\right]^2 0.45(1-0.45)$$

$$= 380.3$$

To estimate the true mean weight to within 10 g with a probability of 95%, would require a sample size of n, where:

$$n = \left[\dfrac{1.96(436.0)}{10}\right]^2$$

$$= 7303, \text{ what a big sample!}$$

7.4 Conclusions

The techniques discussed in this chapter are about making generalising statements describing an unknown population based on information gleaned from a sample of that population. Providing that the sample is collected using one of several mathematically random strategies the formulae given above can be used. The reliability of estimates of characteristics of the population will vary according to the size of the sample and the variability within the sample. A small sample containing a lot of variability will never yield precise estimates of the population.

These concepts are of potential interest to archaeologists. If for example an excavation produced a very large assemblage of flints and available resources did not allow for a full analysis, a randomly drawn sample would allow general statements to be made about characteristics such as means of measurements and proportions of types etc. It is obvious that the emphasis of this approach is on establishing general parameters describing the population and not on identifying and describing unusual and 'special' elements within the population. Of course there is no reason why judgement samples containing obviously special cases can not be taken as well as the random sample so long as it is realised that the aims of the two are different.

It is also not difficult to interpret sampling strategies spatially. An area to be excavated could be gridded into sampling units and the appropriate number selected randomly. Areas of different interest could be built into a stratified design. General parameters of certain aspects of the site can be established using random strategies and this does not preclude the use of the much favoured judgement sampling of areas which look particularly interesting for some reason.

CHAPTER 8

TESTS OF DIFFERENCE

8.1 Introduction.

This chapter is concerned with what are formally called tests of hypothesis for the common statistical parameters. These provide formal methods of answering such archaeological questions as:

(i)   Do the two populations from which these two samples are drawn have significantly different variances (i.e. is there a significant difference in the variability of the weight of sherds of two different pot types?).

(ii)   Could this sample of sherds come from a population that has a mean weight of 250 g?

(iii)   Is the proportion of graves containing a particular type of artefact different between two cemeteries?

The parameters used are calculated from the sample or samples taken and are; the mean, median, variance or standard deviation, proportion and rankings.

In all cases the logic of the test is as explained in Chapter 6. There are many different tests that can be used depending upon the hypothesis to be tested, the assumptions the archaeologist is prepared to make about the data and the size of the samples. Each test is designed for a particular set of assumptions and it can be more difficult choosing the test than actually performing it!

The most important assumption is whether the parent population has a normal distribution or not. If the assumption of normality holds (or can be assumed to hold by virtue of the central-limit theorem (see Chapter 7.3.1)) it is almost certain that a **parametric** test is needed, whilst if it doesn't hold a **non-parametric** test will be appropriate. Parametric tests are generally more powerful because they use the mathematical properties of the normal distribution in distinguishing sets of data. The sample size is another important determinant of the proper test, this is discussed in more detail where appropriate. The examples that follow in this chapter cover both parametric and non-parametric tests for different sample sizes although for certain extreme cases, such as small sample size and non-normality, references are given for more suitable tests.

The first test is described in detail and the rest only briefly since the basic ideas are similar. Whichever test is to be used, therefore, it is recommended that Section 8.2.1 is worked through carefully as it contains many new ideas that are relevant to the other tests.

8.2 One sample tests – comparing an observed measurement with an expected measurement

When a single sample is taken, one of the following two questions is likely to be asked:

(i) Is the average (mean or median) of the sample value significantly different from some fixed value (18 for example).

Note: If it can be assumed that the population from which the sample is taken has a normal distribution, go to Section 8.2.1. If the population is clearly not normal (it is skewed or bi-modal for example), then go to 8.2.2.

(ii) Is the proportion of objects with a certain characteristic significantly different from some fixed value (25% for example). See section 8.2.3.

8.2.1 Test for sample mean

Assumptions: The population has a normal distribution.

Sample statistics used:

n	= sample size
$\bar{x}$	= sample mean
s	= sample standard deviation.

Step 1:

The hypothesis to be tested is often of the type: We have a mean of 18 Type Z sherds per pit from site A, is our sample from site B significantly different? It is usual to denote the fixed value of the mean (18 in this case) as μ_0. The formal statement of both the null hypothesis (H_0) and the alternative hypothesis (H_1) is:

$$H_0: \mu = \mu_0 \qquad \text{vs} \qquad H_1: \mu \neq \mu_0$$

Step 2:

From the sample of n values calculate the sample mean, $\bar{x}$, and the sample standard deviation s. If $\bar{x}$ is very close to μ_0 we will accept the claim that the true mean is μ_0 (accept H_0) but if $\bar{x}$ is very different from μ_0 we should be suspicious and so reject

H_0. The obvious question is, how far can $\bar{x}$ be from μ_0 before we reject H_0? The answer depends upon how large the sample is and how variable the data are.

If the sample variance has been calculated to be s^2, it can be shown that the best estimate for the population variance σ^2 is not s^2 but a slightly modified value (there is not space here to show proofs of this). This best estimate for the population variance is denoted by $\hat{s}^2$ (pronounced s hat squared!) and calculated using:

$$\hat{s}^2 = \frac{n}{n-1}s^2$$

So, if a sample of 10 values gave $s^2 = 1.392$, a better estimate for the population variance would be:

$$\hat{s}^2 = (10/9).\,1.392$$
$$= 1.547$$

This means that if we needed an estimate for the population standard deviation we should use:

$$\hat{s} = \sqrt{\hat{s}^2}$$

$$= \sqrt{1.547}$$

$$= 1.244$$

Clearly if the sample is large, there is little difference between $\hat{s}$ and s (they have similar standard deviations), but for small samples this difference is important.

Many calculators with statistical calculation now give both values for standard deviation. Try with the following data:

Sample: 3, 7, 5, 2

Key on calculator:	n	$\bar{x}$	σ_n	σ_{n-1}
Interpretation:	sample size	mean	s	$\hat{s}$
Contents:	4	4.250	1.920	2.217

In all of the following tests, if these data were to be used, 2.217 would be the appropriate value.

Having gone into some detail on the importance of $\hat{s}$, we can now state the test statistic (TS) to be used:

$$TS = \frac{\bar{x} - \mu}{\hat{s}/\sqrt{n}}$$

Step 3:
If TS is very large we should reject H_0, but accept it if TS is small. We need to define large here – because this is a Two-Tailed Test (see below for explanation) we are talking about absolute values, a TS of −3.9 is just as extreme as a value of +3.9.

To calculate the probability of a TS as large or larger than the value we have arrived at in Step 2 it is necessary to use an appropriate table which has been produced based upon the underlying assumptions. In this case the theory was first developed by W. Gosset in the early 20th century and published under the pseudonym of 'Student' using the symbol t for the test statistic. This is now referred to as the Students t-test or t-distribution, and the associated tables are called t-tables.

Table B in the Appendix is a t-table and it is used frequently later in this chapter. The use of a t-table needs further explanation and a little practice.

Using t-tables:
If we were testing the pair of hypotheses:

$$H_0: \mu = 18 \qquad vs \qquad H_1: \mu \neq 18$$

and a sample size of 6 gave $\bar{x} = 21.9$ and $\hat{s} = 3.0$, then the test statistic would be

$$TS = \frac{21.9 - 18}{3.0/\sqrt{6}}$$

$$TS = 3.18$$

A standard deviation estimated from a sample size n is said to be based upon n−1 degrees of freedom (df) and the appropriate point of entry in the t-table is the row corresponding to the correct df. In this case n = 6 so df = 5, indicating the row to use in the table, (the reasoning behind dfs is involved and not important here). Table B shows:

df	10%	5%	2%	1%	0.1%	df
5	2.01	2.57	3.36	4.03	6.86	5

For 5 df the probability of a TS more extreme than 2.01 is 10%, the probability of a TS more extreme than 2.57 is 5% and more extreme than 3.36 is 2%. Since we have a calculated TS of 3.18, this result is said to be significant at the 5% level but not at the 2% level as it falls between those two values in the table. We can reject H_0 at the 5% level and be 95% confident that the true mean is not 18.

In the example above a TS of −3.18 would lead us to exactly the same conclusion since this would still contradict the assumption that the mean is 18. If the sample mean had been 14.1 rather than 21.9 (3.9 smaller than 18 instead of 3.9 bigger) the TS would be −3.18 rather than 3.18.

This is an example of a **Two-sided Test** or a **Two Tailed Test (TTT)**, we are testing for variation both sides of the true mean, and the logic of this is shown in the following diagram:

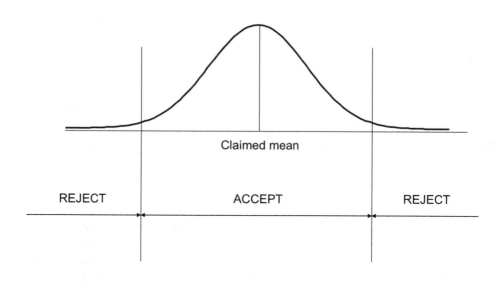

There are many claims that are only one sided, such as "The population mean is not more than 200", giving:

$$H_0: \mu \le 200 \qquad vs \qquad H_1: \mu > 200$$

The logic of this test is:

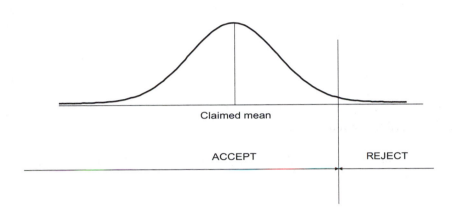

This is an example of a **One-sided** or **One Tailed Test (OTT)** and with such tests care must be taken when using the t-table. If a sample of 13 is taken to test the claim that the population mean is not more than 200 (or is 200 or less), and a TS of 2.91 is calculated, the TS should be compared with those values in the Table B corresponding to **one tail** having probabilities of 5% and 1%. Since the df = 13−1 = 12, we should compare 2.91 with 1.78 (5%) and 2.68 (1%) and so conclude that H_0 can be rejected at the 1% level. We are 99% confident that the mean is more than 200.

Example:
Suppose we were interested in the sockets of spearheads and a previous study had shown that the mean width at the top of the socket was 1.3 cm. Because the original study was carried out a long time ago and the data are not now available, it is of interest to know whether our sample of 40 spearheads are likely to have come from the same population as the originals or not (in other words, are they similar or significantly different). Any variable of interest (on a continuous level of measurement) could be used but in this case we are testing the hypothesis that our sample comes from a population with a mean upper socket width of 1.3 cm. In order to use a t-test we need to assume that the population from which the sample came has a normal distribution. This is a fair claim judging from Figure 6.1. The hypotheses to be tested are:

$H_0: \mu = 1.3$ vs $H_1: \mu \neq 1.3$

[Note: the following is a Test Summary for this test. This format will be followed for all subsequent tests, note that Assumptions is used to include pre-requisits such as minimum sample size.]

One sample test for mean

$H_0: \mu = \mu_0$ vs $H_1: \mu \neq \mu_0$ (TTT)

$H_0: \mu \leq \mu_0$ vs $H_1: \mu > \mu_0$ (OTT)

Assumption: population normally distributed.

Sample statistics needed: n, $\bar{x}$, $\hat{s}$

Test statistic: TS $= \dfrac{\bar{x} - \mu}{\hat{s}/\sqrt{n}}$

Table: t-table (Table B) with df $= n-1$.

This is a two tailed test.

The sample mean and standard deviation for <UPSOC> are calculated to be (using the methods in Chapters 3.4 and 4.5) $\bar{x} = 1.4850$ and $s = 0.3079$.

So,

$$\hat{s} = \sqrt{\frac{40}{39}(0.3079)^2}$$

$= 0.3118$ (this is usually given by σ_{n-1} on a calculator)

and the test statistic:

$$TS = \frac{\overline{x} - \mu}{\hat{s}/\sqrt{n}}$$

$$= \frac{1.485 - 1.3}{0.3118/40}$$

= 3.753 (3 decimal places are enough for any test statistic).

Table B shows that for 39 df for a two tailed test the 5% value is 2.02 and the 1% value is 2.70. Since 3.753 > 2.70, we can reject H_0 at the 1% level and conclude that we have strong evidence (at least 99% certain) that our 40 spearheads come from a population with <UPSOC> different from 1.3 cm. In other words, looking just at this single variable our spearheads are significantly different from those of the earlier study.

8.2.2 Test for median
If the population from which the sample is taken does not have a normal distribution, if it is skewed for example (see Chapter 4.5), this test on the median can be used as a substitute for the test in 8.2.1. Now, however, the key parameter is the median, denoted by θ, rather than the mean.

Note: If n is less than 20, this test is still appropriate although the Binomial tables should be used.

Example:
For the sample of 20 bronze spearheads, the maximum length has a distribution which is not symmetrical as can be seen from the following stem-and-leaf plot:

```
1  01122444
1  66788
2  03444
2
3  0
3  6
```

To test the claim that this sample came from a population with a median of 20 (perhaps this figure has been stated in another report but without the actual data, a comparison would be useful):

One sample test for median

H_0: $\theta = \theta_0$ vs H_1: $\theta \neq \theta_0$ (TTT)

H_0: $\theta \leq \theta$ vs H_1: $\theta > \theta_0$ (OTT)

Assumption: parent population may not be normal, n > 20.

Sample statistics needed: n, T (where T is the number of the n observations which are greater than θ_0).

Test statistic: TS $= \dfrac{2T - n}{\sqrt{n}}$

Table: t-table (Table B) with df $= \infty$ (infinity).

H_0: $\theta = 20$ vs H_1: $\theta \neq 20$ (TTT)

Out of the 20 spearheads it can be seen that 6 have a length of greater than 20 and 14 equal to or less than 20, so T = 6. If the null hypothesis were true we would expect 10 below and 10 above the value of 20, so here we are asking if 6 above the value of 20 is significantly different to 10 above:

Test Statistic = TS $= \dfrac{12 - 20}{\sqrt{20}}$

$$= -1.777$$

Looking at Table B, our result of -1.777 does not reach the 5% value of 1.960 and so is not significant and H_0 cannot be rejected. We should conclude that this sample does not provide enough evidence to reject the claim that it came from a population with a median of 20.

8.2.3 Test for proportions

This test should be used when the proportion of items in a sample with a particular characteristic is under scrutiny. If just one sample is taken it is common to test whether the proportion of interest is different to a particular proportion claimed (larger than or smaller than). This could be applicable to questions such as, "judging from our sample of Wiltshire hillforts are more than 80% of Wiltshire hillforts likely to be multivallate?"

The symbol used to represent proportion is usually π, with π_0 being the claimed proportion and p the observed proportion from the sample.

One sample test for proportions

H_0: $\pi = \pi_0$ vs H_1: $\pi \neq \pi_0$ (TTT)

H_0: $\pi \leq \pi_0$ vs H_1: $\pi > \pi_0$ (OTT)

Assumption: n > 25.

Sample statistics needed: n, p.

Test statistic: $TS = \dfrac{p - \pi_0}{\sqrt{\pi_0(1-\pi_0)/n}}$

Table: t-table (Table B) with df $= \infty$.

Notes:
1) If π_0 is approximately 50%, then this test is valid for samples smaller than 25.
2) If the assumptions are not met (π_0 is not near 50% and n < 25), the Binomial test should be used.

Example:
To test the claim that the proportion of spearheads with a peg hole is **at most** 0.5 (or 50%).

$H_0: \pi \leq 0.5$ vs $H_1: \pi > 0.5$ (OTT)

From the sample of 40 spearheads, 27 have a peg hole so:

$$p = 27/40$$
$$= 0.675$$

Test Statistic = TS $\quad = \dfrac{0.675 - 0.5}{\sqrt{0.5(1 - 0.5)/40}}$

$$= 0.1750/0.0791$$
$$= 2.212$$

Now, from the t-tables (Table B), for a one-tailed test, the 5% critical value is 1.645 and the 1% value is 2.326. Since TS = 2.212, we can reject H_0 at the 5% level but not at the 1% level and conclude that this sample provides significant evidence (we are 95% certain but not 99% certain) that the true population of spearheads with a peg hole is greater than 0.5 or 50%.

8.3 Two sample tests – comparing two observed measurements
8.3.1 Test for variation

If we have two samples, perhaps of different sizes, a common question to ask is if one shows more variability than the other. Variability is usually measured by the variance (see Chapter 5.5) and the essence of this test (formally referred to as the F-test) is to investigate the ratio of the two variances. In this calculation the larger of the two variances is on the top so that if the result is near to 1.0 both variances are considered to be estimates of the same population variance i.e. the samples do not differ in their variability. If, however, this ratio turns out to be large then there is evidence of a difference in variability.

It is usual to use σ^2 for the true variance.

Example:
Out of the 20 bronze spearheads 11 have loops and 9 do not. The weights for these spearheads are as follows:

Loops	No loops
67.7	204.5
170.3	302.4
176.8	623.5
543.2	607.9

628.2	165.6
401.0	307.9
978.9	192.4
111.2	524.7
273.4	178.7
1304.4	
233.8	

Using a calculator gives:

	Loops	No loops
$\hat{s}$	392.9	188.8
$\hat{s}^2$	154,370.4	35,645.44

F-test for variances

$H_0: \sigma_1^2 = \sigma_2^2$ vs $H_1: \sigma_1^2 \neq \sigma_2^2$ (TTT)

Assumptions: two independent random samples from two populations each with a normal distribution.

Sample statistics needed: $n_1, n_2, \hat{s}_1^{\,2}, \hat{s}_2^{\,2}$ (where $\hat{s}_1^{\,2} > \hat{s}_2^{\,2}$).

Test statistic: $TS = \dfrac{\hat{s}_1^{\,2}}{\hat{s}_2^{\,2}}$

Table: F-table (Table C) with df $= n_1 - 1$ and $n_2 - 2$.

It would seem that the weights of spears with loops are much more variable than those without loops. We shall test the hypothesis that the two groups have the same variance (or, if we really want to impress, that they are homoscedastic rather than heteroscedastic!).

$$H_0: \sigma_L{}^2 = \sigma_{NL}{}^2 \quad \text{vs} \quad H_1: \sigma_L{}^2 = \sigma_{NL}{}^2$$

Test statistic $= TS = (154{,}370.4)/(35{,}628.5)$

$= 4.33$

This ratio is large but is it large enough to be significant? To decide this we must consult Table C which shows the 5% critical values for this TS for various combinations of the two sample sizes as df. In this case the df for each sample is sample size minus one, i.e. 10 and 8. The df to be read along the top of the table is that of the sample producing the larger of the two variances (the one on the top of the equation). Here then, we read a df of 10 along the top of the table and 8 down. The 5% value can be seen to be 4.30 and as our TS is slightly bigger than this, H_0 can be rejected at the 5% level. We are 95% confident that there is a difference in the variability of weight between spearheads with and without loops.

8.3.2 Difference in means for paired data – assuming a normal distribution

The socket length and the maximum width for the 11 bronze spearheads with a loop are as shown below, together with the difference (<SOCLE> - <MAXWI>):

Socket length	Maximum width	Difference
4.2	1.8	2.4
3.4	3.3	0.1
6.6	2.7	3.9
7.5	4.4	3.1
8.0	4.5	3.5
8.1	3.5	4.6
5.1	6.0	−0.9
3.6	2.4	1.2
4.8	3.9	0.9
13.5	6.0	7.5
2.4	5.4	−3.0

It seems clear that this group of spearheads have a socket length greater than their width. It is important to realise, however, that because the data are logically paired the method used is to investigate the mean difference (the mean of the differences) rather than the difference in the means (the difference between the mean socket length and the mean width). In this way a large spearhead with a large but similar value for both length and width will not distort the analysis. The method is to calculate the differences and then to carry out a one sample test on the mean of the differences as described in Section 8.2.1.

It is usual to use μ_d for the mean difference for the population and $\overline{d}$ for the calculated mean difference.

Paired samples test for mean difference

H_0: $\mu_d = 0$ vs H_1: $\mu_d \neq 0$ (TTT)

H_0: $\mu_d \leq 0$ vs H_1: $\mu_d > 0$ (OTT)

Assumption: the distribution of the differences is normal.

Sample statistics needed: $n, \overline{d}, \hat{s}_d$.

Test statistic: $TS = \dfrac{\overline{d}}{\hat{s}_d / \sqrt{n}}$

Table: t-table (Table B) with $df = n - 1$.

Example:
To test the claim that bronze spearheads with loops have a socket length greater than their width.

Let d = socket length - maximum width.

H_0: $\mu_d \leq 0$ vs H_1: $\mu_d > 0$ (OTT)

From the 11 differences given earlier, a calculator gives:

$$\overline{d} = 2.118 \text{ and } \hat{s}_d = 2.880$$

and so the Test Statistic is:

$$TS = \frac{2.118}{2.880 \sqrt{n}} \qquad = 2.439$$

From the t-tables (Table B), with 10 df the 5% value is 1.81 and the 1% value is 2.76. Hence H_0 is rejected with 95% confidence and we can conclude that there is significant evidence that for this group of spearheads the socket length is greater than the width, (we cannot, however, be 99% sure of this conclusion).

8.3.3 Difference in means for paired data – no assumptions of normality
In Section 8.3.2 it was assumed that the differences had a normal distribution. If this is not a fair assumption, but it can be assumed that the distribution of the differences is symmetrical (some non-normal distributions are symmetrical), this non-parametric test is suitable.

The differences for each pair are found as before and then ranked (ignoring the sign) and the new ranks given the sign of the original differences. This test is often called a **Wilcoxon Signed Rank Test**. It applies a standard paired t-test (as in Section 8.3.2) to the signed ranks.

Paired samples test – non-parametric

H_0: no difference in the distributions
vs
H_1: distributions are different

Assumptions: the distribution of the differences is symmetrical, $n \geq 10$.

Sample statistics needed: $n, \overline{d}, \hat{s}_d$. Where d = signed rank.

Test statistic: $TS = \dfrac{\overline{d}}{\hat{s}_d / \sqrt{n}}$

Table: t-table (Table B) with df $= n - 1$.

Example:
The same problem as in 8.3.2, gives:

Difference	Rank	Signed rank (d)
2.4	5	5
0.1	1	1
3.9	9	9
3.1	7	7
3.5	8	8
4.6	10	10
−0.9	2.5	−2.5
1.2	4	4
0.9	2.5	2.5
7.5	11	11
−3.0	6	−6

Calculating $\bar{d}$ and $\hat{s}_d$ from the signed rank column gives $\bar{d} = 4.455$ and $\hat{s}_d = 5.359$, and so TS = 2.757 which with 10 df is again significant at the 5% level but not at the 1% level.

8.3.4 Difference in means for two independent samples – assuming a normal distribution

This test is to compare the means from two independent samples, which may be of different sizes. The main assumption is that the two populations from which both samples are taken have normal distributions and equal variances. To test whether the variances are equal use Section 8.3.1.

Example:
For the 20 bronze spearheads, the 10 with peg holes and the 10 without peg holes have the following means and standard deviations for the variable <LOSOC>:

	n	$\bar{x}$	s	s_2	$\hat{s}_2$
Peg	10	2.35	0.196	0.039	0.043
No peg	10	2.01	0.386	0.149	0.166

Is there a significant difference between the two means?

$$H_0: \mu_1 = \mu_2 \quad \text{vs} \quad H_1: \mu_1 \neq \mu_2$$

Two sample t-test

$H_0: \mu_1 = \mu_2$ vs $H_1: \mu_1 \neq \mu_2$ (TTT)

$H_0: \mu \leq \mu_2$ vs $H_1: \mu_1 > \mu_2$ (OTT)

Assumptions: independent samples from populations with normal distributions.

Sample statistics needed: $n_1, n_2, \hat{s}_1, \hat{s}_2$.

Test statistic: $TS = \dfrac{\overline{x}_1 - \overline{x}_2}{\hat{s}\sqrt{1/n_1 + 1/n_2}}$

Where $\hat{s}^2 = \dfrac{(n_1 - 1)\hat{s}_1^{\,2} + (n_2 - 1)\hat{s}_2^{\,2}}{n_1 + n_2 - 2}$

Table: t-table (Table B) with $df = n_1 + n_2 - 2$.

Now, $\hat{s}_2 = \dfrac{(10 - 1)(0.043) + (10 - 1)(0.166)}{10 + 10 - 2}$

$\hat{s}_2 = 0.1045$

$\hat{s} = 0.1045$

$TS = \dfrac{2.35 - 2.01}{0.3233\sqrt{(1/10 + 1/10)}}$

$= 2.35$

With 18 df (10+10−2), the 5% t-value is 2.10 and the 1% value is 2.88. We can reject H_0 with 95% confidence (but not 99%) and conclude that these two samples do provide significant evidence that their means are different.

8.3.5 Difference in means for two independent samples – no assumptions of normality

If the assumption of normality in 8.3.4 is not valid, this non-parametric test is, providing the samples are both of size 10 or more. It is often referred to as the **Mann-Whitney Test** and is a modification of the Wilcoxon Rank Sum Test.

Both samples are put together, ranked, and then the two samples of ranks are analyzed as in the previous t-test (Section 8.3.3).

Difference in means for two samples

H_0: no difference in the distributions
vs
H_1: distributions are different

Assumptions: the distributions are similar except for different means or medians. Two independent samples, both ≥ 10.

Sample statistics needed: $n_1, n_2, \bar{x}_1, \bar{x}_2, \hat{s}_1, \hat{s}_2$. Sample statistics are calculated using the ranks and not the original data.

Test statistic: $\text{TS} = \dfrac{\bar{x}_1 - \bar{x}_2}{\hat{s}\sqrt{1/n_1 + 1/n_2}}$

Where $\hat{s}^2 = \dfrac{(n_1 - 1)\hat{s}_1^{\,2} + (n_2 - 1)\hat{s}_2^{\,2}}{n_1 + n_2 - 2}$

Table: t-table (Table B) with df $= n_1 + n_2 - 2$.

Example:
We shall repeat the test performed in 8.3.4 using <LOSOC> for bronze spearheads to test for a difference between spearheads with a peghole and those without.

Lower socket width		Ranks	
Peg	**No peg**	**Peg**	**No peg**
2.0	1.5	6	1
2.5	2.3	17.5	11
2.4	1.6	14.5	2.5
2.4	2.3	14.5	11
2.1	2.7	7.5	19.5
2.3	2.1	11	7.5
2.2	2.4	9	14.5
2.5	1.8	17.5	4.5
2.4	1.8	14.5	4.5
2.7	1.6	19.5	2.5

Note that the two samples are ranked together, the value of 2.0 has been ranked 6 because it is the sixth smallest out of the whole twenty. Note also that where two or more measurements tie, their ranks are all the same, i.e. the averaged rank. Thus the two spearheads marked with the value 1.6 (no peg) share 2nd and 3rd place, so are ranked each 2.5.

Calculating the Test Statistic using the two rank columns (as in 8.3.4) gives:

$$\bar{x}_1 = 13.15 \text{ and } \hat{s}_1 = 4.58$$

$$\bar{x}_2 = 7.85 \text{ and } \hat{s}_2 = 6.02$$

from which TS = −2.22. Using Table B with 18 df this result is significant at the 5% level but not at the 1% level.

8.3.6 Difference of two proportions
For two independent samples, each of size 20 or more, this test will compare the proportion of objects in one sample which have a certain characteristic, with the proportion from another sample which have a similar characteristic. It is a similar test to that described in Section 8.2.3, with π_1, π_2, p_1 and p_2 being the population and sample proportion of the two samples.

If π_1, π_2 are near to 0.5, then the sample size can be less than 20. If, however, π_1 and π_2 are far from 0.5 both n_1 and n_2 should be at least 25. If these conditions are suspect, Binomial tables should be used to carry out this test.

Difference between two proportions

$H_0: \pi_1 = \pi_2$ vs $H_1: \pi_1 \neq \pi_2$ (TTT)
$H_0: \pi_1 \leq \pi_2$ vs $H_1: \pi_1 > \pi_2$ (OTT)

Assumption: n_1 and $n_2 \geq 20$.

Sample statistics needed: n_1, n_2, p_1, p_2.

Test statistic: $TS = \dfrac{p_1 - p_2}{\sqrt{p(1-p)(1/n_1 + 1/n_2)}}$

where $p = \dfrac{n_1 p_1 + n_2 p_2}{n_1 + n_2}$

Table: t-table (Table B) with df $= \infty$.

Example:
Of the 20 bronze spearheads, 19 were found in Context type 1 (stray finds including hoards) compared to only eight of the 20 iron spearheads. Test the claim that this is a significant difference.

$H_0: \pi_1 = \pi_2$ vs $H_1: \pi_1 \neq \pi_2$ (TTT)

$p_1 = 8/20 = 0.4$

$p_2 = 19/20$

$= 0.95$

Hence:

$$p = \frac{20(0.4) + 20(0.95)}{40}$$

$$= 27/40$$
$$= 0.675$$

Hence:

$$TS = \frac{0.4 - 0.95}{\sqrt{675(1/20 + 1/20)}}$$

$$= -0.55/0.2598$$
$$= -2.117$$

From the t-tables (Table B) with df = ∞, the 5% value is 1.96 and the 1% value is 2.58. Since this is a two-tailed test the sign of the TS is irrelevant, and H_0 is rejected at the 5% but not at the 1% level. We can be 95% sure (but not 99%) that the proportion of bronze spearheads found as stray finds and hoards is significantly different to that for iron spearheads.

CHAPTER 9

TESTS OF DISTRIBUTION

9.1 Introduction

It is quite usual to want to test whether a sample of observations could have come from a particular distribution. For example, the dates of individual artefacts within an assemblage may appear to be random over a time interval of 100 years whilst for a different particular type of object the distribution of dates may seem to be concentrated in the early part of the same period. Are both sets from a similar distribution, is it random, normal or neither?

Many of the tests in Chapter 8 required that the variables had a normal distribution, and if this assumption is in doubt then a formal test to see if a normal distribution is a good fit should be performed. This chapter describes some of the more common **tests of distribution** or **goodness of fit tests**.

The logic behind all these tests is to compare two distributions, the observed distribution and the expected distribution. These two distributions can be visually compared simply by drawing both histograms and this is often enough to allow a conclusion to be made, especially with experience. If in doubt, however, always perform the test.

The following sections describe tests for randomness, normality and between two known distributions.

9.2 Tests of randomness

The dates for our sample of iron spears are between 600 and 1 BC, and a fair question to ask is "are these dates randomly distributed over the range 600 to 0?" If the dates were randomly distributed over this interval then all dates are equally likely and the histogram would be rectangular approximating to Figure 9.1. A random distribution of this type is often called a **rectangular** or **uniform distribution**.

The table below shows the actual distribution of dates for iron spears together with both the cumulative frequencies and the cumulative percentages. From the actual frequencies the histogram shown in Figure 9.2 can be drawn and when this is compared to that in Figure 9.1 there is an obvious difference. In order to test the significance of this difference the **Kolmogorov-Smirnov one sample test** can be used.

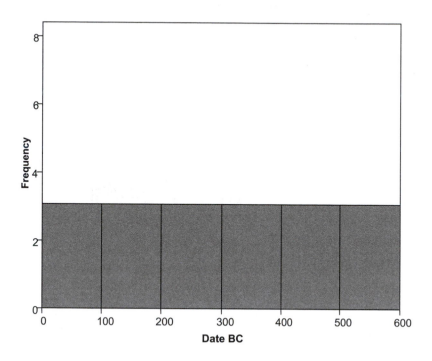

Figure 9.1. A perfect uniform or rectangular distribution.

The essence of this test is to compare the two cumulative distributions (ogives) using a percentage scale for the cumulative frequencies. H_0: Distribution of dates is not uniform on the interval (0,600). The test statistic is the largest difference between these two distributions, ignoring negative signs. This is explained visually in Figure 9.3 which shows both ogives.

The ogive for the expected or hypothesised distribution is simply a straight line joining the two extremes. From Figure 9.3 the maximum difference, D, can be measured to be 22%. Table D (in the appendix) gives critical values for D for varying sample sizes. In this example n=20 (sample size) and so the 5% value is 29.4%. As our figure of 22% is less than the required 29.4% this shows no significant evidence at the 5% level that the distribution of dates is not uniform on the interval (0, 600). In other words H_0 is accepted and the dates are probably randomly distributed.

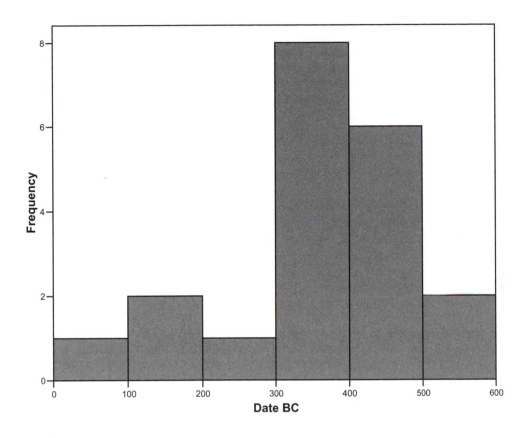

Figure 9.2. A histogram of date, <DATE>.

Date	Frequency	Cumulative frequency	Cumulative %
50	1	1	5
100	1	2	10
150	1	3	15
200	1	4	20
250	0	4	20
300	3	7	35
350	5	12	60
400	3	15	75
450	3	18	90
500	0	18	90
550	0	18	90
600	2	20	100

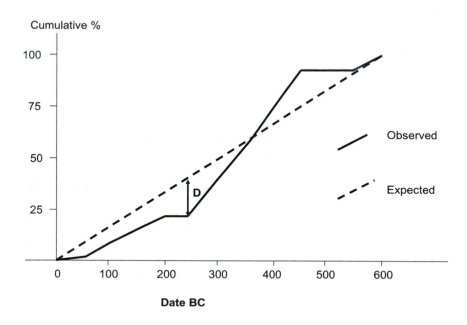

Figure 9.3. The expected and observed cumulative distributions of date, <DATE>.

The comparison of the expected and observed percentages can be made by calculation rather than visually thus giving a more accurate value for D. The following table shows such a calculation producing the result D = 21.7. Here the expected cumulative percentages have been calculated by expressing each date as a percentage of the interval width, 600. 50 as a percentage of 600 is 8.3%. The same row of figures could have been read from the straight line in Figure 9.3, although not as accurately.

Date	Observed cumulative %	Expected cumulative %	Difference
50	5	8.3	3.3
100	10	16.7	6.7
150	15	25.0	10.0
200	20	33.3	13.3
250	20	41.7	21.7
300	35	50.0	15.0
350	60	58.3	1.7
400	75	66.7	8.3

450	90	75.0	15.0
500	90	83.3	6.7
550	90	91.7	1.7
600	100	100.0	0.0

Kolmogorov-Smirnov one sample test of distribution

H_0: population has specified distribution
vs
H_1: population does not have a specified distribution

Assumption: underlying distribution is continuous.

Sample statistics needed: n, cumulative percentages.

Test statistic: D = maximum absolute difference between observed and expected cumulative percentages.

Table: Kolmogorov-Smirnov single sample (Table D).

9.3 Tests for normality

Many of the tests described in Chapter 8 have the assumption that the population from which the sample is taken has a normal distribution. Consequently, an important test to perform is one to decide if the sample could have come from a normally distributed population.

Figure 9.4 shows that the distribution of upper socket width, <UPSOC>, appears to be normal, as was discussed in Chapter 6. If the cumulative percentages of a normally distributed variable are plotted onto special **normal probability graph paper** then a straight line should result. Figure 9.5 is a sheet of such graph paper, and may be photocopied for future use. When the cumulative percentages from the following table for the distribution of upper socket length are plotted on this graph paper, Figure 9.6 shows the results. The straight line indicates that a normal distribution is a good fit for the distribution of <UPSOC>.

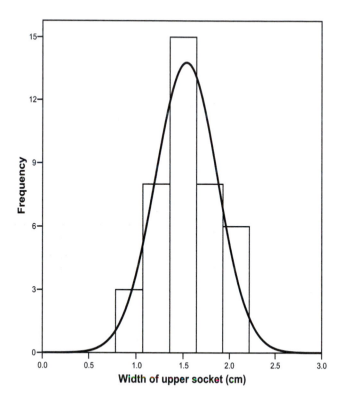

Figure 9.4. A histogram of upper socket length, <UPSOC>.

Upper socket Length	Frequency	Cumulative frequency	Cumulative %
0.55 - 0.75	0	0	0.0
0.76 - 0.95	2	2	5.0
0.96 - 1.15	4	6	15.0
1.16 - 1.35	7	13	32.5
1.36 - 1.55	10	23	57.5
1.56 - 1.75	9	32	80.0
1.76 - 1.95	5	37	92.5
1.96 - 2.15	3	40	100.0
2.16 - 2.35	0	40	100.0

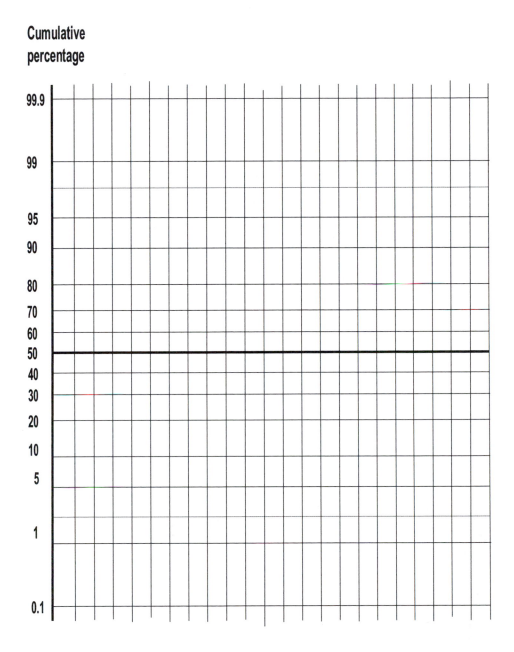

Figure 9.5. Normal probability graph paper.

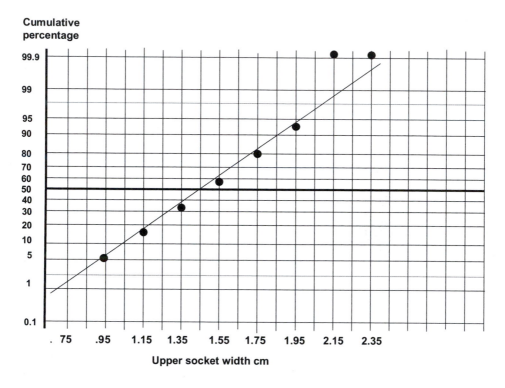

Figure 9.6. Normal probability plot of upper socket length, <UPSOC>.

Using the line plotted in Figure 9.6 can be useful in other ways. Where this straight line crosses the 50% horizontal line is an estimate of the distribution (read from the horizontal axis). The horizontal distance (again using the units of the horizontal axis) from this point to where the drawn line crosses the dotted horizontal lines at approximately 97% and 3% is in each case an estimate for twice the standard deviation. So for this data an estimate for the mean is 1.47 (actual calculated result from the sample is 1.485) and an estimate for the standard deviation is a half of 2.008−1.47, i.e. 0.035 (the sample standard deviation is 0.312).

Consider now the variable maximum length, whose distribution appears not to be normal as shown in Figure 9.7. The following table illustrates the calculation of the cumulative percentages and Figure 9.8 supports the view that a normal distribution may not be a very good model for <MAXLE> because the data do not lie on a straight line when plotted.

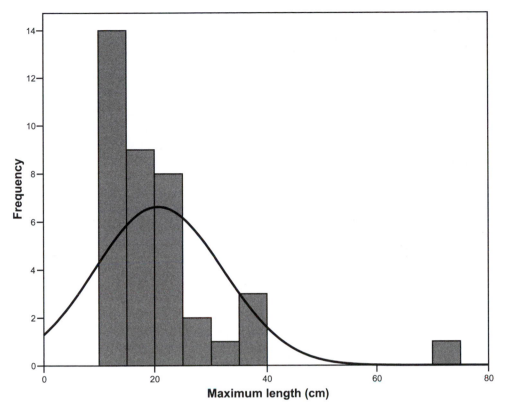

Figure 9.7. A histogram of maximum length, <MAXLE>.

Maximum length	Frequency	Cumulative frequency	Cumulative %
9.9 - 14.9	14	14	36.8
15.0 - 19.9	9	23	60.5
20.0 - 24.9	8	31	81.6
25.0 - 29.9	2	33	86.8
30.0 - 34.9	1	34	89.5
35.0 - 39.9	3	37	97.4
40.0 - 44.9	0	37	97.4
45.0 - 49.9	0	37	97.4
50.0 - 54.9	0	37	97.4
55.0 - 59.9	0	37	97.4
60.0 - 64.9	0	37	97.4
65.0 - 69.9	0	37	97.4
70.0 - 74.9	1	38	100.0

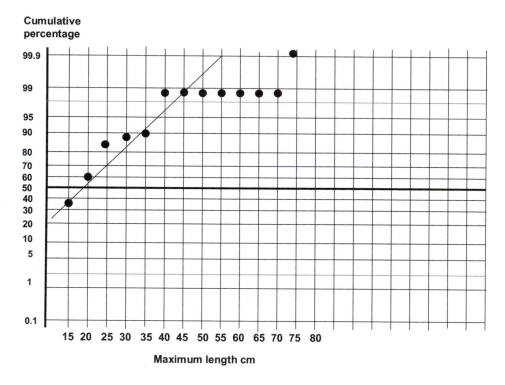

Figure 9.8. Normal probability plot of maximum length, <MAXLE>.

In order to test this conclusion a **Kolmogorov-Smirnov test of normality** should be carried out, which involves comparing the observed cumulative percentages with those expected if the population from which the sample was taken had a normal distribution.

The expected percentages can be read from the straight line drawn on the normal probability graph paper. How this straight line is drawn is critical, look again at Figure 9.8. From the sample the mean and standard deviation can be calculated to be 20.7 and 11.4 respectively. The line is then drawn through the two points at 50% (vertical axis), 20.7 (horizontal axis) and 97%, 43.5. The 43.5 figure is from 20.7 + (2 × 11.4). Reading from Figure 9.8 we get the following cumulative percentages:

Observed	Expected	Difference
36.8	30	6.8
60.5	47	13.5
81.6	64	17.6
86.8	80	6.8
89.5	90	0.5
97.4	96	1.4

110

97.4	97	0.4
97.4	98	1.4
97.4	99	1.6
97.4	100	2.6
97.4	100	2.6
97.4	100	2.6
100.0	100	0.0

The maximum absolute difference between the two cumulative distributions can be read from the table above or from Figure 9.9 and is $81.6 - 64 = 17.6$. Table E shows that for n=38 the 10%, 5% and 1% critical values are 13.0, 14.2 and 16.6 respectively. Since our result is greater than all three of these, there is strong evidence that a normal distribution is a poor fit.

This test assumes that the mean and standard deviation used have been calculated from the sample. If values for the mean and standard deviation are part of the hypotheses or claim, and have not had to be calculated from the sample then Table D should be used.

Kolmogorov-Smirnov one sample test of normality

H_0: population has normal distribution
vs
H_1: population does not have a normal distribution

Assumption: underlying distribution is continuous.

Sample statistics needed: n, mean standard deviation and cumulative percentages.

Test statistic: D = maximum absolute difference between observed and expected cumulative percentages.

Table: Kolmogorov-Smirnov single sample (Table E).

9.4 Tests between two distributions

This section describes how to test a hypothesis that two samples both come from the same population. The following table shows the calculations needed to test the claim that the upper socket width has the same distribution for bronze spears as for iron spears.

Upper socket	Bronze			Iron		
	Freq.	Cum. Freq.	Cum. %	Freq.	Cum. Freq.	Cum %.
0.65 - 0.85	1	1	5	0	0	0
0.85 - 1.05	1	2	10	2	2	10
1.05 - 1.25	2	4	20	3	5	25
1.25 - 1.45	2	6	30	6	11	55
1.45 - 1.65	7	13	65	4	15	75
1.65 - 1.85	4	17	85	3	18	90
1.85 - 2.05	2	19	95	2	20	100
2.05 - 2.25	1	20	100	0	20	100

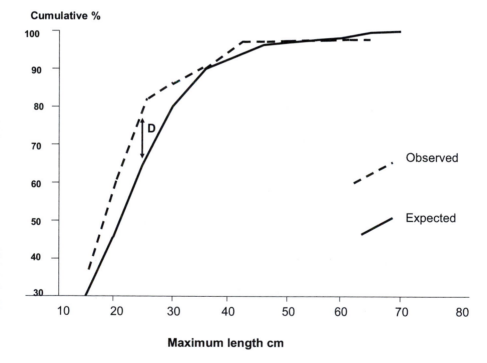

Figure 9.9. Cumulative distribution of maximum length, <MAXLE>.

Here the maximum absolute difference between the two cumulative distributions is D = 25% and this is shown in Figure 9.10 (the 1.25 - 1.45 interval).

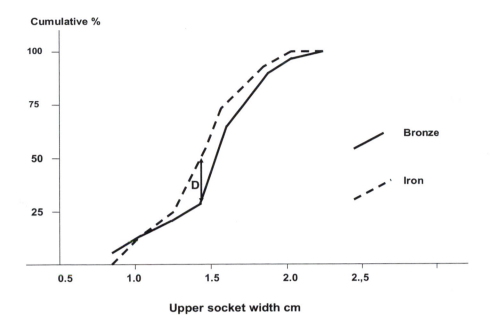

Figure 9.10. Cumulative distributions of socket length, <SOCLE>.

Kolmogorov-Smirnov two sample test

H_0: both samples are from the same population
vs
H_1: samples are from different populations.

Assumption: underlying distribution is continuous.

Sample statistics needed: n_A n_B and cumulative percentages.

Test statistic: D = maximum absolute difference between the two cumulative percentages.

Table: Kolmogorov-Smirnov two sample (Table F).

Table F (in the appendix) is used and the critical values from this table should be compared to:

$n_A.n_B.D/100$ (where n_A and n_B are the two sample sizes).

For these data, $n_A = 20$, $n_B = 20$, $D = 25$ and so:

$20.20.25/100 = 100$

From Table F, the 5% and 1% values are 180 and 220 respectively. Since 100 is less than the lower figure of 180, the result is not significant at even the 5% level and the hypothesis can be accepted. There is no evidence to suggest that upper socket width is different for iron and bronze spearheads in our sample.

CHAPTER 10

MEASURES OF ASSOCIATION FOR CONTINUOUS OR ORDINAL DATA -
ARE TWO VARIABLES RELATED?

10.1 Introduction.
This chapter will discuss the idea of two variables being related, associated or, more properly, **correlated** in a regular way. The variables must be measured on at least an ordinal scale to use these methods. The procedure is to calculate an appropriate correlation coefficient and to then test the significance of the coefficient.

In Chapter 3.5.4 the scatterplot was introduced by showing the relationship between the two variables <MAXLE> and <MAXWI>, this is reproduced here as Figure 10.1.

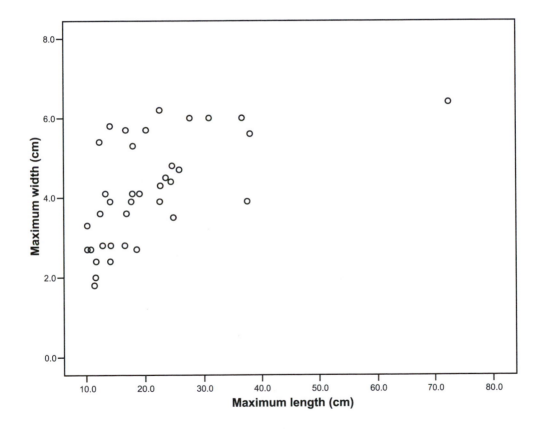

Figure 10.1. A scatterplot of maximum length, <MAXLE>, and maximum width, <MAXWI>.

It shows a reasonably strong relationship between length and width for all 38 spearheads (two have no length recorded as they are broken): generally speaking, as length increases so does width. Figures 10.2 and 10.3 show the relationship between <MAXLE> and <WEIGHT> and <DATE> and <WEIGHT> respectively.

It is clear that there is a very strong correlation between length and weight (Figure 10.2), as expected, but little or no correlation between date and weight (Figure 10.3).

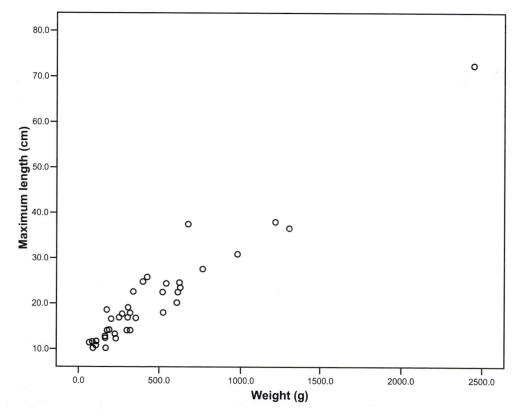

Figure 10.2. A scatterplot of maximum length, <MAXLE>, and weight, <WEIGHT>.

In Sections 10.2 and 10.3 two different methods of calculating a correlation coefficient are presented but in both cases the coefficient has the same interpretation. The usual symbol for this coefficient is r, and it can take values from −1 to +1. A value of +1 indicates a perfect positive correlation (rare in practice), a value of 0 implies no correlation at all whilst −1 shows a perfect negative correlation (as one variable increases the other decreases). These alternatives are illustrated in Figure 10.4.

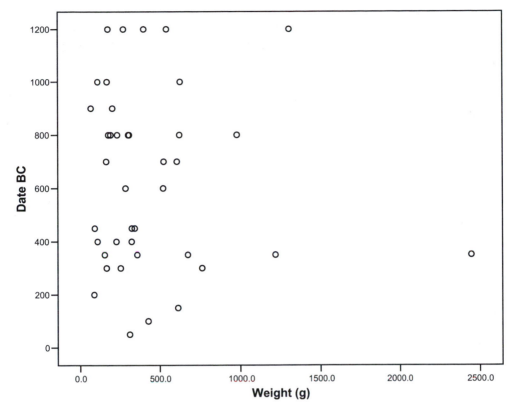

Figure 10.3. A scatterplot of date, <DATE>, and weight, <WEIGHT>.

It is important to realise here that we are talking about linear correlation only (i.e. the tendency towards straight lines in Figure 10.4). There are other types of correlation, more on this later.

If both variables are measured on an interval or ratio scale, then the suitable correlation coefficient is the **Pearson's Product-Moment Correlation Coefficient** and its calculation is described in Section 10.2. For data with one or both variables measured on an ordinal scale, **Spearman's Rank Correlation Coefficient** is the one to use as described in Section 10.3.

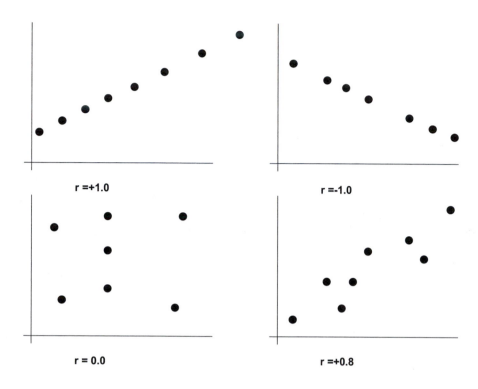

Figure 10.4. Scatterplots illustrating different values of r.

10.2 The product-moment correlation coefficient – two continuous variables

When both variables are measured on either interval or ratio scale, such as weight, length, time, depth etc., then the product moment correlation coefficient (p.m.c.c.) is the best to use. It takes values from between −1 to +1 and has the interpretation discussed in Section 10.1. The calculation of this coefficient is straightforward but tedious.

Calculation:
If the two variables are denoted as x and y, and there are n pairs of observations (x,y), the formula for the p.m.c.c. is

$$r = \frac{n\sum xy - (\sum x)(\sum y)}{\sqrt{[n\sum x^2 - (\sum x)^2][n\sum y^2 - (\sum y)^2]}}$$

Example:
What is the correlation between <MAXLE> and <MAXWI> for bronze spears? Figure 10.5 shows that there is a reasonably strong positive linear relationship - wide spearheads tend to be longer.

Let x = <MAXLE> and y = <MAXWI>. The following table shows all the calculations that are needed for the p.m.c.c.:

x	y	x.x	y.y	x.y
11.4	1.8	129.6	3.24	20.52
16.6	2.8	275.56	7.84	46.48
10.2	3.3	104.04	10.89	33.66
18.6	2.7	345.96	7.29	50.22
24.4	4.4	595.36	19.36	107.36
23.5	4.5	552.25	20.25	105.75
24.8	3.5	615.04	12.25	86.80
14.1	3.9	198.81	15.21	54.99
24.6	4.8	605.16	23.04	118.08
30.9	6.0	954.81	36.00	185.40
20.2	5.7	408.04	32.49	115.14
12.8	2.8	163.84	7.84	35.84
16.9	3.6	285.61	12.96	60.84
14.2	2.8	201.64	7.84	39.76
18.0	5.3	324.00	28.09	95.40
11.7	2.4	136.89	5.76	28.08
14.1	2.4	198.81	5.76	33.84
17.7	3.9	313.29	15.21	69.03
36.6	6.0	1339.56	36.00	219.60
12.3	5.4	151.29	29.16	66.42
Total: 373.6	78.0	7899.92	336.48	1573.21

$$\sum x = 373.6, \sum y = 78.0$$
$$\sum x^2 = 7899.92, \sum y^2 = 336.48$$
$$\sum xy = 1573.21$$
n = 20

$$r = \frac{20(1573.21) - (373.6)(78.0)}{\sqrt{[20(7899.92) - (373.6)^2][20(336.48) - (78.0)^2]}}$$

$$r = \frac{31464.20 - 29140.80}{\sqrt{[157998.40 - 139576.96][6729.60 - 6084.00]}}$$

$$r = \frac{2323.40}{\sqrt{[18421.44][645.6]}}$$

$$r = \frac{2323.40}{\sqrt{11892881.66}}$$

$$r = 2323.40/3448.61$$

$$r = +0.67 \text{ (phew!!)}$$

When similar calculations are performed for iron spearheads the correlation coefficient is +0.57, showing a slightly weaker relationship. For the data in Figure 10.2, $r = +0.96$, and for Figure 10.3, $r = -0.10$.

It has already been mentioned that this correlation coefficient measures linear correlation only and would, therefore, produce a result indicating a poor relationship if the data were as in any of the plots in Figure 10.6.

This would not be a proper interpretation because in each case it can be seen that the data do show strong non-linear relationships. So, be sure of what you are testing for!

Sometimes the **Coefficient of Determination** is used (r^2 or R^2). This can be interpreted as the percentage of variation in one of the variables that is explained by its relation to the other. This can be confusing, but if we look again at <MAXLE> and <MAXWI> for bronze spearheads the coefficient of determination between the two variables is $(0.67)^2 = 0.45$. In other words, 45% of the variation in the length of bronze spearheads can be explained by variation in their width.

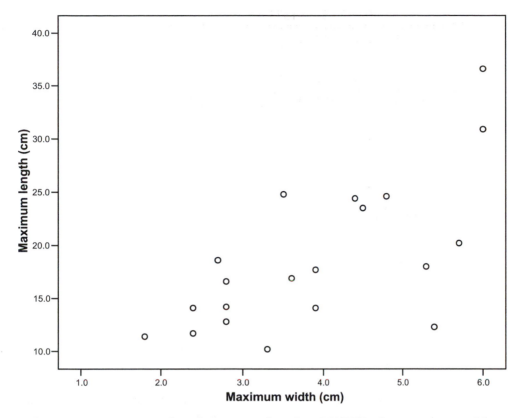

Figure 10.5. A scatterplot of maximum length, <MAXLE>,by maximum width, <MAXWI>, for bronze spearheads.

10.2.1 Testing the significance of the product-moment correlation coefficient.
Having calculated the correlation coefficient it is important to test its significance. In doing this we are attempting to estimate the probability that the true correlation in the whole population from which our sample has been taken is not zero. In other words, is the level of correlation indicated by our sample applicable to the whole population. An important factor to take into account here is sample size.

Obviously, the closer r is to +1.0 (or −1.0) the more confident it is possible to be that there really is a correlation, and this confidence increases as the sample size increases. A value of r = +0.7 calculated from a sample of six pairs is not as significant as a value of r = +0.5 from a sample of 40 pairs. This is because it is quite possible to get a value of 0.7 by chance taking six pairs from a population which in truth has no correlation (r = 0), whilst it is improbable that 40 pairs chosen from the same population would yield a figure of r = 0.5.

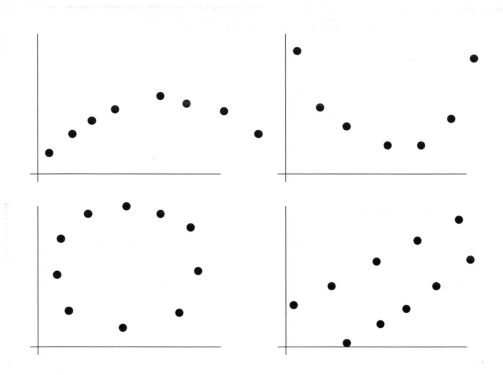

Figure 10.6. Scatterplots showing non-linear relationships.

The usual null hypothesis (see Chapter 6.4 for an introduction to hypothesis testing) for testing the significance of the correlation coefficient is that the population from which the sample has come has no correlation, and the alternative hypothesis is that there is some non-zero correlation (either positive or negative). Appendix Table G is a table showing the critical values of the p.m.c.c. for various values of n, and the test is outlined below.

Example:
To test the significance of the correlation coefficient between <MAXLE> and <MAXWI> for bronze spearheads.

H_0: no correlation between <MAXLE> and <MAXWI> vs H_1: there is some correlation.

Test of product moment correlation coefficient

H_0: true correlation coefficient = 0

vs

H_1: true correlation coefficient $\neq 0$.

Assumption: both variables have approximate normal distributions with similar sized variances.

Sample statistics needed: n, r.

Test statistic: TS = r.

Table: product moment correlation coefficient table (Table G).

The sample of 20 pairs gave r = 0.67. From Table G it can be seen that for N = 20 the probability of a coefficient higher than 0.444 (or lower than −0.444) is less than 5%, and the probability of a coefficient higher than 0.561 (or lower than −0.561 is less than 1%. As our figure of 0.67 is above the 1% figure we can state that our result is significant at the 1% level.

In other words, H_0 can be rejected at the 1% level and it is at least 99% certain that there is some correlation between <MAXLE> and <MAXWI>.

10.3 Spearman's rank correlation coefficient – two ordinal variables

If one or both of the variables under investigation is measured on an ordinal scale, or if they do not have an approximately normal distribution, then Spearman's rank correlation coefficient (noted as r_s) is suitable. It is much easier to calculate than the p.m.c.c., and is often used for this reason even when the data justify the use of the latter. The values of r_s have a similar interpretation to those of r.

Calculation:

The first step is to replace each of the two variables by ranks, starting from 1 for the smallest in each case. If two observations tie for a rank position they both take the mid-point, if, for example, there is a tie for third place both take the rank of 3.5. The difference in the two rank positions for each pair is calculated and called d. Spearman's rank correlation coefficient is given by:

$$r_s = 1 - \frac{6\sum d^2}{n(n^2 - 1)}$$

An example always helps!

Example:
Since the variable <DATE> may be rather subjective it is best treated as an ordinal variable. To calculate the correlation between <DATE> and <WEIGHT>, therefore, Spearman's correlation coefficient can be used as follows:

Date	Weight	Date (rank)	Weight (rank)	d	d^2
300	167.0	6.0	5	1.0	1.00
450	342.1	17.0	12	5.0	25.00
400	322.9	14.0	10	4.0	16.00
350	154.8	10.0	4	6.0	36.00
350	358.1	10.0	13	−3.0	9.00
400	227.9	14.0	6	8.0	64.00
450	323.8	17.0	11	6.0	36.00
600	285.2	19.5	8	11.5	132.25
150	613.8	3.0	16	−13.0	169.00
300	254.3	6.0	7	−1.0	1.00
50	310.1	1.0	9	−8.0	64.00
100	426.8	2.0	14	−12.0	144.00
600	521.2	19.5	15	4.5	20.25
300	765.1	6.0	18	−12.0	144.00
350	1217.2	10.0	19	−9.0	81.00
350	2446.5	10.0	20	−10.0	100.00
350	675.7	10.0	17	−7.0	49.00
450	90.9	17.0	2	15.0	225.00
200	86.8	4.0	1	3.0	9.00
400	109.1	14.0	3	11.0	121.00
				Total:	1446.50

Since $\sum d^2 = 1446.5$, n = 20

$$r_s = 1 - \frac{6(1446.5)}{20(20^2 - 1)}$$

$$= 1 - \frac{8679.0}{20(399)}$$

$$= 1 - 8679.0/7980.0$$
$$= 1 - 1.09$$
$$r_s = -0.09$$

This shows a very weak correlation between date and weight, (look back to Figure 10.3).

Caution:
If there are many ties in the rankings the above calculation should strictly be modified to allow for this. As this modification is complicated it will not be included here in detail, with the modification the corrected value of r_s for the above is -0.10. Most statistical software packages automatically apply this modification when required, but it could be that the methods described in Chapter 11 are more appropriate anyway.

Figure 10.7 shows the relationship between <WEIGHT> and <SOCLE> for iron spearheads (there are only 19 points because one is broken).

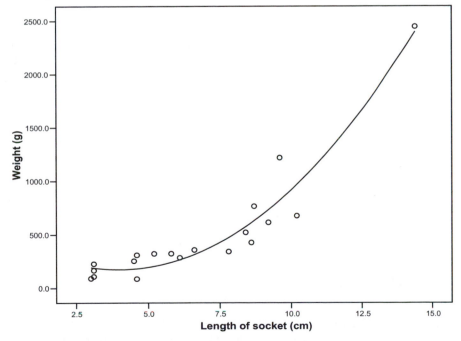

Figure 10.7. A scatterplot of weight, <WEIGHT>, and socket length, <SOCLE>, for iron spearheads.

There is a strong relationship which is not quite linear and is best described by the curve drawn. Using p.m.c.c. r = 0.86, this understates the strength of the relationship whereas Spearman's rank coefficient gives $r_s = 0.94$, a fairer value. This is partly due to the problem of outliers (such as the one in Figure 10.7) and the way that the p.m.c.c. will incorporate **all** points in its calculation. This means that a few, or even just one, outlier can have a great effect on the result. If outliers cannot be eliminated from the analysis on sound archaeological grounds, Spearman's could be more appropriate even if both variables are ratio.

10.3.1 Testing the significance of Spearman's rank correlation coefficient.
The steps and the logic are just as for the p.m.c.c:

Test of Spearman's Rank correlation coefficient

H_0: true correlation coefficient = 0
vs
H_1: true correlation coefficient $\neq 0$.

Assumption: both variables at least ordinal.

Sample statistics needed: n, r_s.

Test statistic: TS = r_s.

Table: Spearman's Rank correlation coefficient table (Table H).

Example:
Is the value of $r_s = -0.09$ obtained for <DATE> and <WEIGHT> significant?

H_0: true correlation = 0   vs H_1: true correlation $\neq 0$

The lowest level of significance we are prepared to accept is the 95% level. Table H shows that for n = 19 to be at least 95% confident of some correlation requires r_s to be either more than 0.460 or less than −0.460. Our calculated r_s of −0.09 is too close to zero and so H_0 cannot be rejected; H_0 is accepted. There is no significant evidence of any correlation between date and weight.

10.4 Predicting using regression.

Closely related to correlation is regression. This is the technique of deriving an equation to predict one variable from another having shown them to be correlated. The example here is a simple one that predicts the value of one variable from one other. A more complicated example is described in Chapter 12, one that uses the combination of several variables to predict another variable's value, the multivariate technique of Multiple Regression.

The theory of regression is beyond the scope of this book although once the concepts of correlation are mastered, regression can be approached using one or more of the recommended books (see Chapter 13), most statistical software will also produce regression results (see Chapter 14).

Consider the length of iron spearheads, <MAXLE>. Of the 20 in our data-set two have no measurement for this variable probably because they are broken. Can we predict what their lengths would have been? The correlation (p.m.c.c.) between <MAXLE> and <SOCLE> is 0.90, showing that <SOCLE> is a good predictor for <MAXLE>, (in fact, 81% of variation in <MAXLE> is explained by <SOCLE>). The result of regression analysis is the following regression line predicting <MAXLE> from <SOCLE>:

Predicted <MAXLE> = −5.65 + 4.26(<SOCLE>)

For spearhead Number 8, socket length = 6.1 and so predicted maximum length
= −5.65 + 4.26(6.1)
= −5.65 + 25.99
= 20.34 cm.

The other missing length cannot be predicted since it has a missing socket length

CHAPTER 11

MEASURES OF ASSOCIATION FOR CATEGORICAL DATA – ARE TWO CHARACTERISTICS RELATED?

11.1 Introduction.

This chapter discusses methods of measuring and testing for association between two variables, where one or both are measured by belonging to a categorical classification or range, (see Chapter 1.2 for discussion on levels of measurement). If both variables are measured on interval or ratio scales, that is they are continuous such as weight or length, then the techniques in Chapter 10 are more suitable. Note that continuous variables can be converted to categorical by recoding them; length, for example, could be classified into short, medium and long.

Typical examples of questions that could be asked using the tests of this chapter on categorical data are:

(i)   The sherds from an excavation have been classified into types according to form and counts made of each type for each site phase. Is there any association between type and phase?

(ii)   A collection of flints can each be uniquely allocated to one of three sources by chemical analysis and each flint is from one of five geographical areas. Is there any association between find area and source?

(iii)   For our sample of spearheads, is there any association between the material of the spear and whether it has loops?

For all such problems the first step is to display the data in a contingency table (see Chapter 3.3.2 for an introduction to contingency tables), in which each cell contains the frequency (or count) for that particular combination of the values. The following is a contingency table for the spearhead data showing the cross-tabulation of material and the presence of loops:

Material	Loops		
	No loop	Loop	
Iron	20	0	20
Bronze	9	11	20
	29	11	40

This is a 2 by 2 (or 2 × 2) contingency table with the marginal frequencies shown indicating that out of the 40 spearheads, 29 did not have loops, 20 were bronze etc.

So far so good - but beware! Here an often confusing situation must be introduced because there are two distinct questions that can be, and may be, and often are, asked:

1. Is there any association between the two variables?
2. How strong is the association between the two variables?

It is possible to have a data set that provides strong statistical evidence (i.e. it is significant) of a weak association. These are two totally different concepts and should be kept separate, bear them in mind as this chapter progresses and things may get clearer!

The choice of technique to be used here depends upon the quality (level of measurement) of the data and the sample size. The most common test is that described in the next section, Chi-squared, while Sections 11.3 and 11.4 present two other useful ones from the many more available. Correspondence Analysis (Chapter 12) expands these ideas.

11.2 The Chi-squared test – the commonest method.

The **Chi-squared Test**, developed by Karl Pearson in 1900, is a suitable technique to ascertain if the data contained in a contingency table provides significant evidence of an association between the two variables. Chi-squared is suitable for data measured at the nominal or ordinal levels although with ordinal data the technique described in Section 11.4, Kendall's Tau, is more powerful and more suitable.

The Chi-squared test is a method of comparing the observed frequencies (the data) with those expected under the null hypothesis of no association (or independence) between the two variables. These expected frequencies are calculated using the marginal frequencies in the contingency table.

If we return to the 2 × 2 table in the section above showing material and the presence of loops, if there had been no association between material and loops we would expect a proportion 20/40 to be bronze. That is, instead of an observed frequency of 11, we expect 11(20/40), which is 5.5. This seems to show that in our sample of 40 spearheads, bronze spearheads tend to have loops. The essence of a Chi-squared test is to compare all of the observed frequencies (denoted by O) with each of their corresponding expected frequencies (denoted by E).

Calculation:
Step 1:
calculate all of the expected frequencies using the marginal frequencies. Apply the following rule to each cell:

$$\text{Expected frequency} = \frac{\text{(row total)/(column total)}}{\text{(overall total)}}$$

So the expected frequency for the iron/loop cell is:

$$\frac{(20)(11)}{(40)}$$

$$= 5.5$$

The following table shows all of the expected frequencies (in brackets) together with the observed frequencies:

Material	Loops		
	No loop	Loop	
Iron	20 (14.5)	0 (5.5)	20
Bronze	9 (14.5)	11 (5.5)	20
	29	11	40

Step 2:
calculate the test statistic using the Chi-squared statistic:

$$\chi^2 = \sum \frac{(O-E)^2}{E}$$

where χ^2 is the Greek letter Chi (c in English)
O is the observed frequency
E is the expected frequency
and the summation is over all the cells, i.e. in this case four.

The calculation of χ^2 is best set out in a table as follows:

O	E	O−E	$(O-E)^2$	$(O-E)^2/E$
20	14.5	5.5	30.25	2.09
0	5.5	−5.5	30.25	5.50
9	14.5	−5.5	30.25	2.09
11	5.5	5.5	30.25	5.50
				Total = 15.18

Hence $\chi^2 = 15.18$

Now, if χ^2 is very large, this indicates a large difference between the observed and expected frequencies and so there would be significant evidence of association. A very small χ^2 near to 0, would provide no evidence of association. To decide whether or not a calculated χ^2 is significant use Table I (in the Appendix), having first calculated the degrees of freedom (d.f.) for the contingency table under investigation.

The d.f. for a table with r rows and c columns (r × c table) are:

d.f. = (r−1)(c−1)

so for this 2 x 2 table:

d.f. = (2−1)(2−1)
= (1)(1)
i.e. d.f. = 1

Table I then shows that for 1 d.f. the critical 5% value is 3.84, the 1% value is 6.63 and the 0.01% value is 10.8. The calculated χ^2 value for our problem is 15.18 which allows the null hypothesis to be rejected at the 0.1% level. There is significant evidence of an association between material and the presence/absence of loops.

Important note 1:
For a 2 × 2 table the Chi-squared statistic as described above is often modified to provide a more conservative test. This modification, called Yates' continuity correction, is automatically applied by most statistical software. It involves reducing the absolute size of the difference O−E by subtracting 0.5 before squaring. Had this been done for the previous example the corrected χ^2 would have been 12.54, slightly smaller but still providing significant evidence of an association.

Important note 2:
For the Chi-square test to be valid all of the expected frequencies should be 5 or more. In practice, however, this can be relaxed for tables larger than 2 × 2 to be no more than 20% of all cells should have expected frequencies less than 5. Under no circumstances should any expected frequency be less than 1. It may be possible to either omit categories with low expected cell counts or to combine categories. These decisions should be based on archaeological reasoning and justification – the statistics should serve the archaeology and not the other way around. Guttman's lambda (see Section

11.3) is a test of association that can be used when several of the cells have low or even zero counts.

Test of association – Chi-squared

H_0: no association

vs

H_1: some association

Assumption: no more than 20% of all expected frequencies are less than 5.

Sample statistics needed: observed cell frequencies for a contingency table (r × c).

Test statistic: $\chi^2 = \sum \dfrac{(O - E)^2}{E}$

Where:
E = expected cell frequencies if H_0 is true
O = observed cell frequencies

Table: Chi-squared (Table I) with (r − 1) (c − 1) degrees of freedom.

Example:

To test if there is an association between material and date, a 2 × 3 contingency table is made by splitting date into three (arbitrary) period categories, producing the following table:

Material	Date (period)			
	Late (50-399)	Middle (400-799)	Early (800-1200)	
Bronze	0	3	17	20
Iron	12	8	0	20
	12	11	17	40

H_0: no association vs H_1: is association

The expected frequency to correspond to the observed frequency of 3 (bronze spearheads of the middle 'period') is $(11)(20)/40 = 5.5$.

Repeating these calculation steps (as shown in detail above) yields a Chi-squared of 31.27 which is based upon $(2-1)(3-1) = (1)(2) = 2$ degrees of freedom. Using Table I, H_0 can confidently be rejected, or, the result is significant at the 0.1% level. There is strong evidence of an association between material and period as categorised here.

The Chi-square statistic tells us whether the two variables are related (associated), its size indicates the strength of the evidence for this association. Now we must confront the complication mentioned at the beginning of this chapter. So far we have answered the first of the two questions; is there any association between the two variables? The second question of interest, what is the strength of the association between the two variables, can now be answered.

After calculating Chi-squared and showing it to be significant, for there is no point in progressing to the second question if there is no evidence of an association, another statistic called Cramer's V can be calculated to measure the strength of the association. This is defined by:

$$V = \sqrt{\frac{\chi^2}{(n)(m)}}$$

where:
n = the total of all the frequencies, (the total number of cases or objects) and m = the smaller of $(c-1)$ and $(r-1)$, (r and c are the number of rows and columns)

V takes a value between 0 and 1 with values close to 1 indicating a strong relationship.

Examples:
For the first table considered above, the 2×2 table of material by presence/absence of loops, $\chi^2 = 12.54$, n = 40 and m = 1, so

$$V = \sqrt{\frac{12.54}{(40)(1)}}$$

$$= \sqrt{0.134}$$

$$V = 0.56$$

For the second table, material by period (2 × 3), $\chi^2 = 31.27$, n = 40 and m = 1, so

$$V = \sqrt{\frac{31.27}{(40)(1)}}$$

$$= \sqrt{0.782}$$

$$V = 0.88$$

Although in both cases there is significant evidence of an association, there is a stronger association between material and period than there is between material and loop.

11.3 Guttman's lambda – an alternative

Guttman's lambda is a measure of association with the advantage of being applicable when several of the cells have low or even zero counts. It is presented here simply as a measure of association rather than as a test.

To measure the association between the variables <COND> and <CON>, the starting point is the following contingency table:

Context	**Condition**				
	Excellent	Good	Fair	Poor	
Stray/hoard	8	15	4	0	27
Settlement	0	2	2	2	6
Burial	0	1	3	3	7
	8	18	9	5	40

Imagine trying to predict the context from the condition. If it was in good condition the best guess would be that it was from a stray find/hoard context, but if it was in poor condition the best guess would be a burial context since this has the highest frequency. If this logic had been used for each of the four categories of condition we would have made 8+15+4+3 = 30 correct guesses. If, on the other hand, we knew nothing about condition but still wanted to predict context we would have guessed stray/hoard as this is the most popular of the three, and in this case there would have been only 27 correct guesses. Thus by knowing the condition we have increased the number of correct guesses by 30–27 = 3.

Guttman's lambda, often written λ, is the ratio of this increase to the total number of incorrect guesses (the number here is 40–27 = 13),

i.e. $\lambda = 3/13$
$= 0.231$

There is another way λ can be defined, this time by trying to predict condition from context rather than the other way around:

$$\lambda = \frac{(15 + 2 + 3) - 18}{40 - 18}$$

$$\lambda = \frac{20 - 18}{22}$$

$$\lambda = 0.091$$

Both of these values of lambda are said to be **asymmetric** because one variable (the **dependent** variable) is being predicted from the other (the **independent** variable). A **symmetric** value of λ can be defined as a sort of average of the two asymmetric values, and in this case is:

$$\lambda \,(\text{symmetric}) = \frac{(30 - 27) + (20 - 18)}{(40 - 27) + (40 - 18)}$$

$= 5/13$
$= 0.143$

These results show that knowing the condition of a spearhead does increase the chance of guessing or inferring the context (λ with context dependent $= 0.231$) but that the reverse relationship is not so strong (λ with condition dependent $= 0.091$).

11.4 Kendall's tau.
If both variables are measured on an ordinal scale, then **Kendall's tau** is more appropriate (more powerful) than Chi-squared. It can be used even if many of the cell counts are zero or low. An interval/ratio scale variable that has been grouped into classes of increasing value is also suitable (the values of <MAXLE>, for example, could be grouped into long, medium and short).

Beware! This situation is not always clear-cut, a codified pottery classification, for instance, is not ordinal unless there are incontrovertible archaeological reasons for uniquely associating each class of pottery with an ordered scale. The obvious example is a typology where clear temporal development is believed so that the scale is one of time.

Kendall's tau, often written τ (Greek again!), can take values from -1 to $+1$ and has a similar interpretation to the correlation coefficients described in Chapter 10. There are two versions of tau, **tau-c** and **tau-b**, tau-c is for tables which are not square, eg. 2×3 or 4×5, whilst tau-b is for square tables, 3×3 etc.

Example 1 (tau-c):
Consider again, measuring the association between date (split into three periods) and material, as discussed in Section 11.2. By calculating Chi-squared we obtained V = 0.88, showing a strong association. Both variables are ordinal (a dichotomy can be considered to be ordinal, see Chapter 1.2), and so although Chi-squared can be used, Kendall's tau is more appropriate as a measure of association because it uses more of the information contained in the data (i.e. the ordering).

Material	Date (period)			
	Late (50-399)	Middle (400-799)	Early (800-1200)	
Bronze	0	3	17	20
Iron	12	8	0	20
	12	11	17	40

Since this is a 2×3 table tau-c is appropriate.

$$\text{tau-c} = \frac{2k(P - Q)}{n^2(k-1)}$$

where:
    n = the total frequencies (cases, objects)
    k = the smaller of the number of rows or columns
    P = the sum of each cell frequency multiplied by the sum of all the frequencies below and to the right. Don't panic! This is much simpler than it sounds, see the example below.
    Q = the sum of each cell frequency multiplied by the sum of all the frequencies below and to the left.

For this table:
    n = 40
    k = 2 (from 2×3)

P = 0(8+0) + 3(0) + 17(0) + 12(0) + 8(0) + 0(0) For each cell the figures in brackets are the cell counts below **and** to the right of it in the table

P = 0 + 0 + 0 + 0 + 0 + 0

P = 0

Q = 0(0) + 3(12) + 17(12+8) + 12(0) + 8(0) + 0(0)

Q = 0 + 36 + 340 + 0 + 0 + 0

Q = 376

Hence:

$$\text{tau-c} = \frac{2(2)(0-376)}{40^2(2-1)}$$

$$= \frac{4(-376)}{1600}$$

$$= -1504/1600$$
$$= -0.94$$

Whereas the result from the Chi-squared test showed a strong association (V = 0.88), this result uses the ordering in the data to indicate a strong **negative** association (or correlation) thereby producing a more informative outcome. Iron is clearly later than bronze!

Example 2 (tau-b):
To measure the association between material and the presence/absence of loops, since both variables are dichotomous we can treat them as ordinal:

Material	Loops			
	No loop	Loop		
Iron	20	0	20	
Bronze	9	11	20	
	29	11	40	

For this square table tau-b is appropriate:

$$\text{tau-b} = \frac{P - Q}{\sqrt{(P + Q + TR)(P + Q + TC)}}$$

where:

P and Q are as for tau-c
TR = the sum of each frequency multiplied by the total of all the frequencies which are to the right and in the same row.
TC = the sum of each frequency multiplied by the total of all the frequencies which are below and in the same column.

Hence:

$$P = 20(11)$$
$$= 220$$

$$Q = 0(9)$$
$$= 0$$

$$TR = 20(0) + 9(11)$$
$$= 99$$

$$TC = 20(9) + 0(11)$$
$$= 180$$

therefore:

$$\text{tau-b} = \frac{220 - 0}{\sqrt{(220 + 0 + 99)(220 + 0 + 180)}}$$

$$= \frac{220}{\sqrt{(319)(400)}}$$

$$= +0.62$$

This confirms the reasonably strong association between material and presence/absence of loops suggested by the earlier Chi-squared result ($V = 0.56$).

Both lambda and tau have appropriate tests of significance. They are not described here because they involve complex mathematics and the use of specialised tables. It will be found, however, that most statistical computer software will produce a probability value with the results for these measures of association. Using the explanations of the concepts of probability and significance testing from earlier chapters, such results should make some sense.

CHAPTER 12

AN INTRODUCTION TO MULTIVARIATE ANALYSIS

In earlier chapters we have seen examples of univariate analysis using such techniques as simple bar charts, frequency tables of one variable and calculations of a simple sample mean. When two variables are involved such as in clustered bar charts, scatterplots, when we are comparing the mean of two groups or when we are asking is there any association between two variables, then we are using techniques of bivariate analysis. More than two variables, however, and we are dealing with multivariate analysis, such as in Chapter 3, Figure 3.11 which shows three variables on one scatterplot, a very simple example.

In this chapter we take this idea further and will introduce you to some of the common techniques of multivariate analysis that can be, and have been, applied to archaeology. We concentrate on what sort of relationships they can be used to investigate (i.e. what sorts of archaeological questions can be asked), what sort of data is needed as input and how to interpret the basic output.

These techniques require the use of suitable statistical packages because of the considerable computation involved. Consequently, the approach of working examples by hand used in earlier chapters is not relevant here and we will not be going into the statistical and mathematical details behind the techniques, nor will we discuss all of the output that modern statistical packages produce. This is intended as a simple introduction to some multivariate techniques to demonstrate their potential. If you are going to use these techniques we recommend that you consult one or more of the appropriate books listed in Chapter 13. There are many published examples of using multivariate analysis in archaeology going back many decades resulting in a considerable body of literature and experience.

The techniques discussed here fall into two broad types:

Type A: reduction and grouping. Given several measurements (ordinal interval or presence/absence) on each of many objects (i.e. several variables and many cases) is it possible to reduce the number of variables, still maintaining the information in the data? Using either the original variables or the new reduced set can these objects be put into groups or clusters so that within each group the objects are similar but between groups there are interpretable differences. Techniques to be used:
Cluster Analysis
Correspondence Analysis
Principal Components and Factor Analysis

Type B: prediction. Given several measurements (ordinal interval or presence/absence) on each of many objects (i.e. several variables many cases) with one of the variables of particular interest, is it possible to predict this variable from the others and if so which variables are important in this prediction? Techniques to be used:
Multiple Regression
Discriminant Analysis

12.1 Reduction and grouping
12.1.1 Cluster Analysis
Can the spearheads be put into groups, or clusters, so that those within a cluster are similar to each other but there are important differences between the clusters? How many such clusters are there? Cluster Analysis was one of the first popular statistical applications in archaeology because it relates to the process of classification. Large bodies of material can be divided up into groups based on their physical characteristics. The subjectivity in this procedure, as in all other multivariate techniques, lies in the choice of variables to use and in interpreting the output, in this case what number of clusters is 'significant'. Another important choice when using Cluster Analysis is which method to use, the principles of the technique are demonstrated here through the use of a single method.

Most packages offer the standard clustering method called **hierarchical cluster analysis** which starts by putting each case (spearhead) into its own cluster so that there are many clusters each with one member. Having been told how the similarity between clusters or cases is to be measured and what the rules are for combining clusters (see below), the software will reduce the number of clusters by one at each step until there is just one big cluster. The output will provide information on cluster membership at each stage and indicate how good the clustering has been (i.e. how 'similar' the members of each cluster are). The following example illustrates some of these ideas by trying to cluster the spearheads using only the two main size measurements of maximum length and maximum width, shown in Figure 12.1 as a scatterplot.

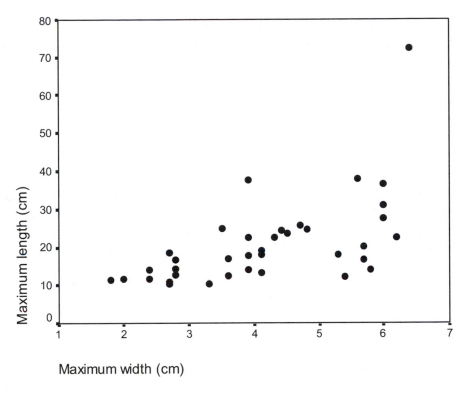

Figure 12.1 A simple scatter plot of length <MAXLE> by width <MAXWI>

One of the choices to be made is how to measure the similarity between the clusters and probably the simplest is by using the distance between them (the Euclidean distance). The other choice is how to join, or agglomerate clusters, and probably the commonest method is to join those two clusters where the similarity between their averages is smallest. This is referred to as Average Linkage. So, using these two decisions i.e. Euclidean distance and Average Linkage, the following three figures, 12.2, 12.3 and 12.4, show the cluster membership when there are 2, 3 and 4 clusters. Note that using our two chosen variables, this means that spearheads of similar size will be considered similar, even if they have a different shape (i.e. cluster membership is based entirely on maximum length and maximum width).

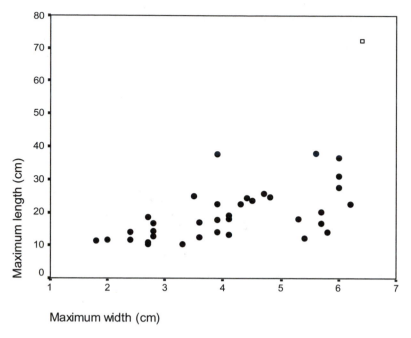

Figure 12.2 Euclidean distance 2 Clusters

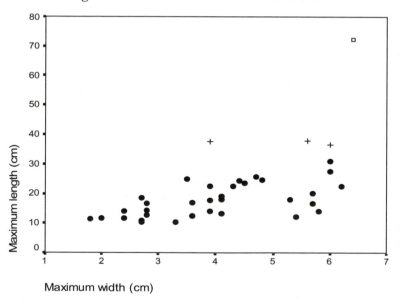

Figure 12.3 Euclidean distance 3 Clusters

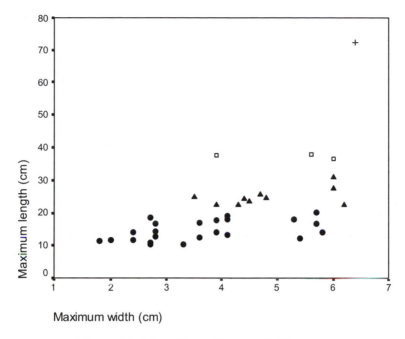

Figure 12.4 Euclidean distance 4 Clusters

Clearly large spearheads are being grouped together and it appears that length is having a greater influence than width, probably because it is usually much bigger. To avoid this, the data can be standardised (by using z-scores, see Chapter 5) and Figure 12.5 shows cluster membership for 4 clusters this time using z scores. Although the result is very similar, it does provide a 'more balanced' use of the two variables and is preferable to that from the raw data.

When the relative shape (rather than just size) is important, so that ⌂ and

are considered similar, then Cosine (rather than Euclidean distance) is a

better method of measuring similarity as it is a type of correlation coefficient. Figure 12.6 shows the results of using Cosine which has clearly produced a very different set of clusters. As mentioned above, the choice of which method to use is for the archaeologist to decide and will usually be based on the nature of the objects themselves and, perhaps, on which method produces the most interpretable results.

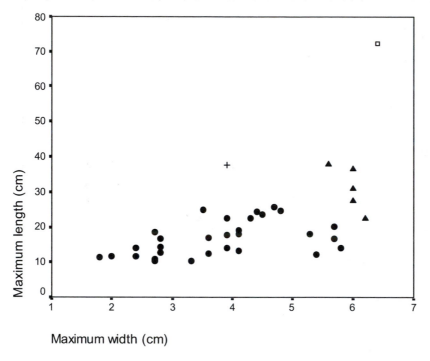

Figure 12.5 Standardised Euclidean distance 4 Clusters

The way to 'visualise' the clusters as they are formed, as an aid to deciding how many are 'significant', is by asking the software to produce **a dendrogram**. This is a diagram that shows which objects joined to which others and at what stage. A dendrogram for clustering based upon length and width using Euclidean distance is shown in Figure 12.7. It can be seen that spear number 16 does not join with any other spears until the distance to join is quite high so clearly spear 16 is an odd one out (it is the very big one). Also spears 15, 39 and 17, although similar to each other (relatively long), are different from both spear 16 and all the others. So, ignoring spear 16 there are three clear clusters (grouped as 10 to 40, 25 to 30 and 15 to 17 on the dendrogram working downwards) and this is reflected in groupings within the scatterplot of Figure 12.4.

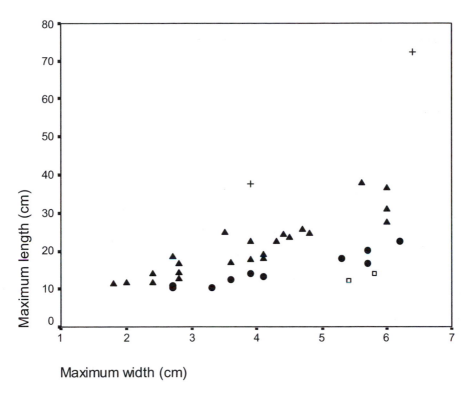

Figure 12.6 Cosine similarity 4 Clusters

12.1.2 Correspondence Analysis

In Chapter 11 contingency tables were used to answer the question "is there any association between two categorical variables, such as Material and Loop?" The data in Table 12.1 produced a Chi-squared value of 15.18 which was highly significant allowing the conclusion that there is strong evidence that the presence/absence of a loop is associated with material. The nature of this association is evident from the 2×2 table which shows that Iron spears do not have loops.

Material	Loops		
	No loop	Loop	
Iron	20	0	20
Bronze	9	11	20
	29	11	40

Table 12.1 Contingeny table for MATERIAL <MAT> and LOOP <LOO>

145

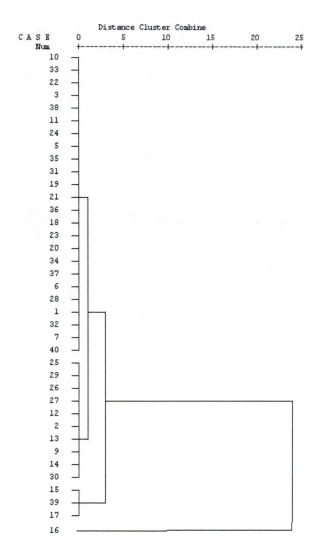

Figure 12.7 Dendrogram using Euclidean distance

This is fairly straight forward for 2×2 tables but when each of the two categorical variables has more that two categories, it is often not clear by looking at the table what the association is, even if this association has been shown to be significant. In such situations Correspondence Analysis can aid the interpretation of any associations, or correspondences, in a contingency table. Of course, the categorical variables used could be different ranges of a continuous variable.

146

The statistics underlying this are based on the idea that, for example, the data in a table with 3 rows and 4 columns can be represented by using $(3-1)(4-1) = 6$ new variables or dimensions. If these new variables are chosen optimally then the first two of them may represent much of the overall variation between the 12 different categories. A scatterplot showing these two new variables or dimensions will then make clear any associations. This sounds rather vague and to avoid getting deeper into mathematical statistics it is simpler to just rely on a statistics package to produce such a plot. So, what is the relationship, if any, between Condition and Context?

| | | Context | | | |
		Stray find	Settlement	Burial	Total
Cond	Excellent	8	0	0	8
	Good	15	2	1	18
	Fair	4	2	3	9
	Poor	0	2	3	5
Total		27	6	7	40

Table 12.2 Crosstabulation of Condition <COND> and Context <CON>

Table 12.2 is the contingency table and it is not obvious what the associations are if any. When a correspondence analysis is run using these two variables, the main output is the chart as shown in Figure 12.8

It can be seen clearly here that finds in excellent and good condition are more likely to be stray finds whilst burials tend to produce finds in only fair condition and settlements are not strongly associated with finds in any particular condition.

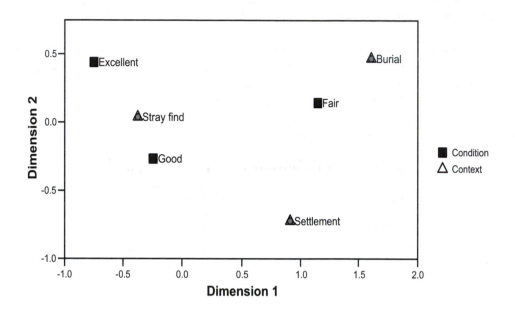

Figure 12.8 Correspondence plot for context <CON> and condition <COND>

Essential to this process is the reduction of several variables to being represented by two new variables. In the example above the two categorical variables of condition and context had essentially 12 different categories (3×4) and Correspondence Analysis reduced these to two (Dimensions 1 and 2 in the plot). If the original variables were all measured on interval scales (rather than categorical) then the techniques of **Principal Components Analysis or Factor Analysis** would be used to reduce the number of variables to ease interpretation. In Principal Components Analysis the result will indicate how many new transformed variables are needed to satisfactorily explain the data. Factor Analysis is very similar although the user states how many new transformed variables, or factors, are required. While we are not going into the detail of these two techniques here, if both were applied to the interval variables of the spearhead data they would show that maximum length and width are the two most important variables for describing the spearheads.

12.2 Prediction
12.2.1 Multiple Regression
Can the length of a spear be predicted if the tip is missing? Section 10.4 demonstrated how this could be achieved through simple regression using one other variable to

predict length, in that case socket length. It worked quite well because the two variables were initially shown to be correlated. A more sophisticated approach to regression is the multivariate technique of Multiple Regression which predicts based on information from more variables.

Multiple Regression will produce a linear equation relating spear length, the **dependent variable**, to several **independent variables** such as socket length, maximum width, width of upper socket and width of lower socket. Both the dependent variable (the one to be predicted) and the independent variables (the ingredients for this prediction) must be measured on an interval scale or be presence absence data. The results for this regression are shown in Table 12.3

Variable	Coefficient	t	sig
(Constant)	−10.823	−1.884	.068
<SOCLE>	2.924	7.124	.000
<MAXWI>	1.703	1.964	.058
<UPSOC>	6.177	1.772	.086
<LOSOC>	−1.483	−.435	.666

Table 12.3. The Regression of Length

This means that to predict length we use the following equation (taken from the values in the Coefficient column of the table):

Length = −10.823 + 2.924 × Length of socket + 1.703 × Maximum width + 6.177 × Width of upper socket −1.483 × Width of lower socket

The high t values and the corresponding low significance probabilities confirm that the constant term and the first three variables play a significant role in predicting length. However, the low t value and high significance value for 'Width of lower socket', <LOSOC>, suggests that this last variable contributes little of any significance once the earlier three are used. It could be left out of the equation (or model) and Table 12.4 shows the output for this new reduced model.

Variable	Coefficient	t	sig
(Constant)	−12.025	−2.417	.021
<SOCLE>	2.896	7.232	.000
<MAXWI>	1.611	1.939	.061
<UPSOC>	5.335	1.863	.071

Table 12.4 The new regression of Length

Here the new equation is:

Length = −12.025 + 2.896 × Length of socket + 1.611 × Maximum width + 5.335 × Width of upper socket

There is much extra output from any package running multiple regression, of which the most important is the value given for the **Coefficient of Determination** which measures the percentage of the overall variation in the dependent variable explained by the model. This coefficient is often written R^2 with $R^2_{adjusted}$ being a slightly better version. For the first model used here with all four independent variables these coefficients are:

$R^2 = 0.884$ $R^2_{adjusted} = 0.754$

For the reduced model with only three independent variables they are:

$R^2 = 0.883$ $R^2_{adjusted} = 0.760$

The simpler equation is better because $R^2_{adjusted}$ is bigger and shows that 88% of the variation in length is explained by the model based on the variables 'Length of socket', 'Maximum width' and 'Width of upper socket'.

Figure 12.9 is a simple scatterplot showing that this model can predict length quite well by comparing actual lengths with predicted lengths.

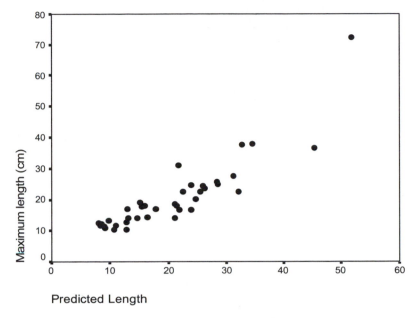

Figure 12.9 Scatter plot of Maximum length against Predicted length

If, for example, there was a spear with a broken tip but with measurements of 10.1, 7.3 and 2.2 for 'Length of socket', 'Maximum width' and 'Width of upper socket', then the predicted length would be:

Predicted Length = −12.025 + 2.896(10.1) + 1.611(7.3) + 5.335(2.2)
Predicted Length = 40.72

12.2.2 Discriminant Analysis
If the context of a spear is unknown, can its original context be predicted from the values of its other variables? This is a similar question to that of predicting length but here the variable to be predicted takes only three values (it is categorical). Whenever the variable to be predicted is either dichotomous (takes one of two values, for example presence/absence data), or takes one of only a few different categories, then Discriminant Analysis is better than Multiple Regression. Again the dependent variable (to be predicted) and the independent variables must be measured on an interval scale or be presence absence data.

Be warned – Discriminant Analysis output can include some extremely confusing tables but probably the easiest part of a typical output to understand is the classification summary. Table 12.5 is an example for predicting Context and shows that nearly 90% of all contexts have been correctly predicted from the spears' other characteristics. Note also that all the burials (6 in total) have been correctly predicted. This means that a spear with no known context can have its context predicted with some confidence.

		Context	Predicted Group Membership			Total
			Stray find	Settlement	Burial	
Original	Count	Stray find	25	1	1	27
		Settlement	1	3	1	5
		Burial	0	0	6	6
	%	Stray find	**92.6**	3.7	3.7	100.0
		Settlement	20.0	**60.0**	20.0	100.0
		Burial	.0	.0	**100.0**	100.0

89.5% of original grouped cases correctly classified.

Table 12.5 Discrimination results for predicting Context <CON>

Like Multiple Regression, Discriminant Analysis allows for the predicting variables to be interpreted and reduced or added to in order to improve the prediction. Table 12.6 shows the contribution each variable has made to the two discriminating functions needed to define the three categories of Context (note that if there were only two categories, including presence/absence, then only one function is needed). These results show that Maximum Length and Weight are important discriminators (high values whether positive or negative) whilst Upper Socket Length is not.

With large data files it is a good idea to develop the predictive model by using only part of the data, perhaps a random sample of 70%, and to then test it on the remainder. The results for the other 30% can be predicted and tested against the actual values, most packages have this facility built into them.

	Function	
	1	2
<MAT>	−.533	.360
<LOO>	.497	1.105
<PEG>	.340	.839
<COND>	−.703	−.051
<MAXLE>	1.802	4.145
<SOCLE>	−.730	.382
<MAXWI>	−.145	1.414
<UPSOC>	.181	−.179
<LOSOC>	−.075	.621
<MAWIT>	1.005	−1.472
<WEIGHT>	−1.280	−4.602

Table 12.6 Standardised Discriminant Function Coefficients for predicting Context
<CON>

Points to remember:
Treat multivariate techniques with caution – they will always provide an 'answer' (i.e. some form of output) whether or not it makes any archaeological sense.

The simple examples above only give a flavour of some multivariates – use the appropriate books from Chapter 13, and/or software documentation, and/or a friendly statistician.

Experiment by changing input variables and parameters in a gradual way so that changes in output can be monitored, tracked and interpreted. There is nothing wrong with experimenting and this may well help to understand the patterns and relationships within complex data sets.

CHAPTER 13

A FEW RECOMMENDED BOOKS

The aim of Digging Numbers is to encourage archaeologists to start using statistics rather than just reading about statistical applications in archaeology. To try and emphasise this we have decided not to include references and a detailed bibliography of quantitative methods in archaeology, but instead, to recommend a few specific titles which can be used in support of the techniques presented herein.

First of all, for complete beginners:

Improve Your Maths
G Bancroft & M Fletcher, 1998, Addison-Wesley; ISBN0201 331306
If your basic mathematics needs improving so that you can perform simple algebraic manipulations and numerical calculations, then this is the book for you.

Of general use:

Dictionary of Statistics and Methodology
W P Vogt, 1999, Sage; ISBN0761912746
Each entry has a brief but clearly explained definition with occasionally a more thorough explanation. There is a good reference section for further reading.

These days many statistical books are based on using a particular computer package, here are a selection for SPSS:

Discovering Statistics using SPSS for Windows
A Field, 2000, Sage; ISNB 07619 57553
A nice book that covers most of the topics in Digging Numbers and uses SPSS. Written in an easy to read style and sometimes quite humorous, the underlying theory is explained but not given mathematically. It is a good text to use as a follow up for this book since it extends topics such as Regression, Experimental Design (ANOVA) and Factor Analysis. There is no coverage of Cluster Analysis or Correspondence Analysis though. SPSS data files are supplied on a CD.

Analyzing Quantitative Data
N Blaikie, 2003, Sage; ISBN0 7619 67583
This book is about how to use quantitative data to answer research questions in social research. Although clearly aimed at social researchers it expends the topics in Digging Numbers with good explanations, little mathematics and may be favoured by the less

technical archaeologist. There is an Appendix which gives very brief instructions for using SPSS.

SPSS for Windows Made Simple Release 10
P R Kinnear & C D Gray, 2000, Psychology Press; ISBN 1 84169118
A large book mainly concentrating on how to use SPSS but with some discussion of the underlying concepts behind each technique. Goes further than Digging Numbers on Factor Analysis, Loglinear models and ANOVA but has nothing on Cluster Analysis or Correspondence Analysis. Does contain good exercises for each chapter.

Archaeological statistical books at an introductory level:

Mathematics in archaeology
C R Orton, 1980, Collins; ISBN 052128922X
An old book and now out of print but still worth reading if you can get hold of it. This is an excellent introduction to the sorts of archaeological questions that can be asked and answered through the use of mathematics and statistics.

Statistics for Archaeologists. A commonsense approach
R D Drennan, 1996, Plenum Press; ISBN 0306453266.
A good, clear introduction to univariate and bivariate methods with the emphasis on Exploratory Data Analytical approaches. Also includes good sections on sampling and correlation.

Multivariate analysis in archaeology:

Exploratory Multivariate Analysis in Archaeology
M J Baxter, 1994, Edinburgh University Press; ISBN 0 7486 0423 5
A thorough coverage of Principal Component Analysis, Correspondence Analysis, Cluster Analysis and Discriminant Analysis with a general introduction and good coverage of the literature on multivariate applications.

Quantifying Archaeology (2nd Edition).
S Shennan, 1997, Edinburgh University Press; ISBN 0748607919
Covers the whole range of univariate, bivariate and multivariate techniques including a good discussion of sampling. Many worked examples based on archaeological problems.

Multivariate Archaeology. Numerical Approaches in Scandinavian Archaeology
T Madsen (ed), 1988, Jutland Archaeological Society; ISBN 8772880473
Probably out of print and not a text book as are the above, but still a very useful collection of papers specifically about Correspondence Analysis. If you are going to use this

technique seriously then this collection should be consulted to get a good grasp of the range of archaeological applications that are appropriate.

More specific areas of archaeological statistics:

Sampling:

Sampling in Archaeology
C R Orton, 2000, Cambridge University Press; ISBN 0521566665.
A thorough coverage of sampling including the history of sampling in archaeology, the full range of techniques and applications, and a new approach called adaptive sampling. Includes many archaeological examples and statistical detail in an Appendix.

Spatial statistics:

Spatial analysis in archaeology
I Hodder and C Orton, 1976, Cambridge University Press; ISBN 0521210801
Out of print but still the 'classic' as an introduction to spatial statistics and their potential in archaeology. Good discussion of principles, point and grid differences and the main techniques such as Nearest-Neighbour and Trend Surfaces.

Intrasite spatial analysis in theory and practice
P H Blankholm, 1991, Aarhus University Press; ISBN 8772883294
A thorough coverage of spatial techniques applied to archaeological problems, a 'manual' approach. The computing aspects of the book are now out of date but still worth a look if you are going to do spatial statistics.

Intrasite Spatial Analysis in Archaeology
H Hietala (ed), 1984, Cambridge University Press; ISBN 0521 250714
Another old book probably out of print but still a useful collection of papers illustrating the range of applications of spatial statistics in archaeology.

Bayesian statistics:

Bayesian Approach to Interpreting Archaeological Data
C E Buck, W G Cavanagh, and C D Litton, 1996, John Wiley and Sons; ISBN 0471961973
A thorough coverage of the complex world of Bayesian statistics with the emphasis soundly on archaeological applications. Describes the Bayesian approach to probability, statistical modelling, bivariate, multivariate and spatial distributions. Interesting sections addressing archaeological questions such as sourcing and provenancing and dating.

Archaeological statistical software:

Other than the wide range of commercial statistical software packages, there are a small number of specifically archaeological ones. Probably the most widely used (in the UK at least) are:

the Bonn Archaeological Statistical Package (BASP), see
http://www.uni-koeln.de/~al001/basp.html [accessed 19th September, 2004]

and **MV-ARCH**, see
http://acl.arts.usyd.edu.au/acl/products/software_utilities/mvarch/mvnuts.html
[accessed 19th September, 2004]

CHAPTER 14

SPSS for WINDOWS

14.1 Chapter 1: an Introduction to SPSS and data

The Statistical Package for the Social Sciences (SPSS) is a suite of computer programs, which has been developed over many years. Its aim is to make data entry, statistical presentation, statistical analysis, and interpretation easy. These notes are written for SPSS v12 (although elements will be valid for earlier versions).

Steps in statistical analysis using SPSS

Step 1

Enter the data into SPSS and check accuracy.

1. Open a saved SPSS data file, or
2. Export from a spreadsheet file, or
3. Enter data directly via Data Editor.
4. Check the data for slips etc

Step 2

Select a procedure from the menus.

1. Statistical analysis; e.g. mean, correlation.
2. Create a chart.

Step 3

Select variables for the analysis.

1. Dialog boxes display variables.
2. Select variables and run analysis.

Step 4

Examine and interpret the results.

1. Results displayed in output window.
2. Charts displayed in Chart Carousel.
3. Charts can be modified.

When you start an SPSS session, the data window and applications window open automatically.

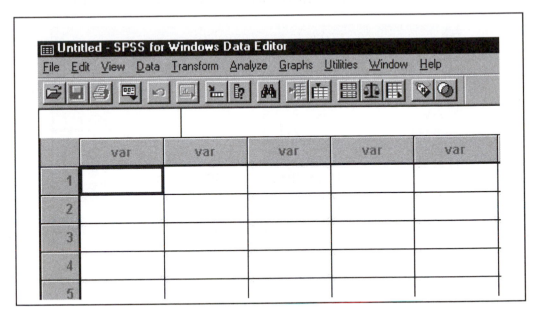

Use menus and the tool bar to select files, statistics and charts.

FILE - Open, Save, Print data output and charts

EDIT - Modify, cut, copy and paste, and search for text and data

DATA - Define, sort, and select data; merge files

TRANSFORM - Transform data values, compute new variables with arithmetic expressions

ANALYSE - Run statistical analysis; results are displayed in the output window

GRAPHS - Create charts; charts are displayed in the Chart Carousel

UTILITIES - Get variable and file information; change fonts, display value labels in Data Editor

WINDOW - Arrange and select windows

HELP - For assistance; press F1 or Shift F1

Dialog Boxes

Dialog boxes are used to select variables and options for statistics and charts.

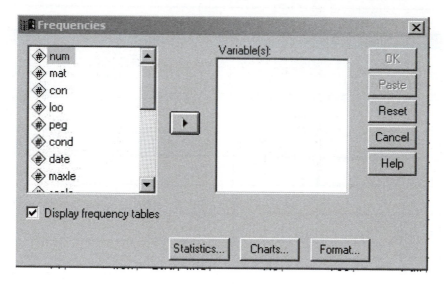

Variables for analysis are selected from a source list.

Use the arrow button to move the variables into the target list.
The variables may be listed by either the variable name or any variable labels. The default is to list by variable label. If this is not wanted then change by using Edit/Options/General/ and alter the setup at the top right.

Subdialog boxes can be opened for optional selections.

SPSS has an extensive online help system. Select HELP from the SPSS menu bar. Alternatively press F1 button.

If you need help on how to use a dialog box, then use the HELP button.

Data

In SPSS for Windows, data is usually entered via the Data Editor Window. A SPSS data file is similar to a spreadsheet except for a few differences:

a) Each row is a single case (e.g. one spearhead from the total list of spearheads)

b) Each column is a single variable (a piece of relevant information, e.g. maximum length)

c) Each cell contains a value defined by its row and column location

d) A missing value is indicated by a full-stop (.)

File Edit View Data Transform Analyze Graphs Utilities Window Help

1 : num | 1

	num	mat	con	loo	peg	cond	date
1	1	Iron	Burial	No	Yes	Fair	300
2	2	Iron	Burial	No	Yes	Poor	450
3	3	Iron	Burial	No	Yes	Poor	400
4	4	Iron	Burial	No	0	Poor	350
5	5	Iron	Burial	No	No	Fair	350
6	6	Iron	Burial	No	Yes	Fair	400
7	7	Iron	Burial	No	Yes	Good	450
8	8	Iron	Settlement	No	Yes	Poor	600
9	9	Iron	Settlement	No	Yes	Poor	150
10	10	Iron	Stray find	No	Yes	Fair	300
11	11	Iron	Stray find	No	Yes	Good	50
12	12	Iron	Stray find	No	Yes	Fair	100
13	13	Iron	Stray find	No	Yes	Good	600
14	14	Iron	Stray find	No	Yes	Fair	300
15	15	Iron	Stray find	No	Yes	Good	350
16	16	Iron	Stray find	No	Yes	Good	350

SPSS Data Types
Within SPSS you can enter data as various data types:

Numeric: data which is numerical in form. The display format indicates the class width and the number of decimal places; e.g. 8.2 indicates that a total of 8 spaces is allocated to each value and all values will be displayed to two decimal places (e.g. 3 will be displayed as 3.00).

String: SPSS does accept string (alphanumeric) data. There are drawbacks to using string variables. First, typing them in takes longer than typing numbers. Second there are limitations on what SPSS can do with them.

Date: 4th June 2005 will be recorded as 04.06.05

However, in general, it is always best to enter data in a Numeric form. String data can usually be entered in numeric form, with an appropriate label. For example, Material is defined as Bronze or Iron. It is probably better to record the data as 1 and 2 and then provide value labels

> 1 = Bronze
> 2 = Iron

Opening an existing SPSS file is straightforward:

> Select FILE from Menu Bar
> Select OPEN from FILE menu
> Select DATA from OPEN submenu
> Type in filename or select from the list of files
> Click on OK

Open SPEARS.SAV which can be obtained from
> www.soc.staffs.ac.uk/mf4/spears.zip

Having opened this file do the following tasks:

Click on **label** on toolbar to identify value labels.

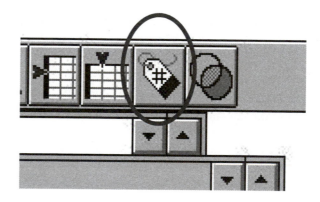

Increase the width of some columns by putting the cursor on the divider between the variable names and dragging.

Double click on the 'cond' variable, change the name to 'condition', look at the variable name, value labels (Values), data type, missing values and column format. An alternative is to change to Variable View (bottom left of SPSS window).

Double click on the '**cont**' variable to investigate the column format and the display format.

> Exit the SPEARS.SAV file by
> Selecting FILE from the menu bar
> Selecting EXIT from the file menu
> (You have a choice as to whether to save any changes.)

This causes SPSS to be closed down.

Entering data via the data editor
Entering simple numeric data is easy - select the appropriate cell and enter the number, then press enter. You must be in Data View, bottom left of SPSS screen. If you haven't named the variable, SPSS assigns a unique **variable name**. However, it is best to assign an appropriate name (variable names are best kept short) by double-clicking at the top of the column and entering the name and use the dialog boxes to provide a **variable label**, (display label) and **display format.**
Example:

Variable name -	MAXLE
Label -	Maximum length (cm)
Display format -	4.1 (Width 4 with 1 decimal place e.g. 12.4)

Remember, to enter a variable name double click at the top of the column (or select **Insert variable** from the Data menu, which will open the Variable view.

Enter the relevant information for material in your data set in the second column in the following way:

Variable name -	MAT
Label -	material

Now define the **Value labels**.

With a grouping variable comprising a set of arbitrary code numbers, it is useful to assign value labels showing what these numbers represent. Choose Variable View and then click on Values. With the **Value Labels dialog box** on the screen, type *1* into the value box and in the **value label box** type *Bronze* using the tab button to move to the value label box. This will embolden the **Add** button. When **Add** is clicked,
> 1 = '**Bronze**'
will appear in the lowest box. In a similar manner, proceed to label the value 2, so that
> 2 = '**Iron**'

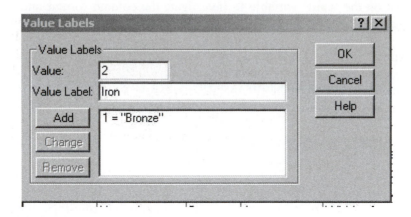

Return to the Data Editor by clicking on OK.
Now name and label the remaining information that was collected.

When all the data is in save it by choosing:
File
Save as

Editing, saving and printing data
The Data Editor offers a range of functions, some of which are extremely useful not only for amending data that are already in the grid but also for inputting data values that are repeated many times.

Changing isolated values in the grid
Enter a few numbers in the grid. Any of these can be changed at will by targeting the cell concerned with the black rectangle, typing a new value and pressing **enter**.

Blocking
Initially, only one cell is highlighted. It is possible, however, to highlight a whole block of cells. This **blocking** operation is achieved very simply by clicking and dragging and using the copy and paste commands. This is useful, for example, if you have a large number of consecutive 'Burial' spearheads in your sample.

	num	mat	con	loo	peg	cond	date	maxle
1	1	Iron	Burial	No	Yes	Fair	300	12.4
2	2	Iron	Burial	No	Yes	Poor	450	22.6
3	3	Iron	Burial	No	Yes	Poor	400	17.9
4	4	Iron	Burial	No	0	Poor	350	.
5	5	Iron	Burial	No	No	Fair	350	16.8
6	6	Iron	Burial	No	Yes	Fair	400	13.3
7	7	Iron	Burial	No	Yes	Good	450	14.1
8	8	Iron	Settlement	No	Yes	Poor	600	.
9	9	Iron	Settlement	No	Yes	Poor	150	22.5
10	10	Iron	Stray find	No	Yes	Fair	300	16.9
11	11	Iron	Stray find	No	Yes	Good	50	19.1
12	12	Iron	Stray find	No	Yes	Fair	100	25.8
13	13	Iron	Stray find	No	Yes	Good	600	22.5
14	14	Iron	Stray find	No	Yes	Fair	300	27.6

Saving the data set

Having gone to considerable trouble to enter the data into the Data Editor, the user will wish to save them in a form that can be called up instantly at the next session, rather than having to type in all values again. To save the data to a file, proceed as follows after making sure that the data is visible in the open window. In the SPSS Application window, choose:

File

Save As

this obtains the **Save Data As** dialog box

In the File Name text box, is ***.sav**. Enter into the **File Name box** any name with extension **.sav** (e.g. testdata.sav). Restrict the name to eight characters.

Note that if you wish to save the data onto floppy disk then enter

a:\testdata.sav

in the filename box.

Transforming variables.

SPSS has several ways that data can be transformed, all using the **Transform** function at the top of the **Data View** screen. To create the new variable 'Period' from the existing variable Date first select **Transform/Recode/Into Different Variable** as below:

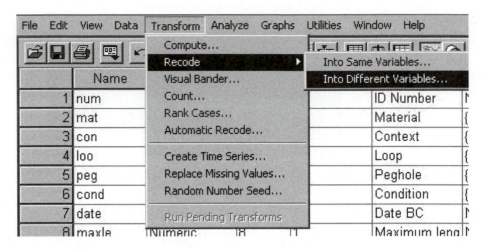

This then produces a window asking for the name of the new variable (period).

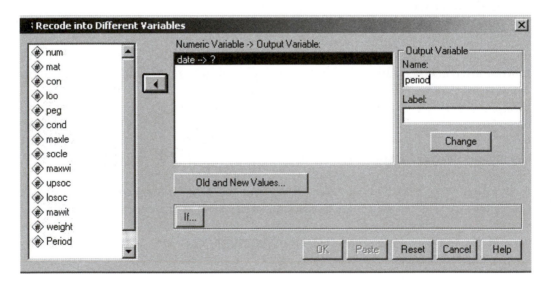

After choosing **Change** choose **Old and New Values** to get this window:

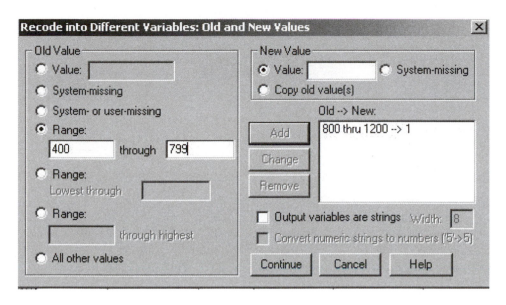

On the left input the old values and on the right the new ones using **Add** to add the transformations into the right hand box. Continue followed by **OK** will complete the transformation.

To see this new variable either look at your data - it will be a new column on the right or use **Analyse/Descriptive Statistics/Frequencies** as in the following windows.

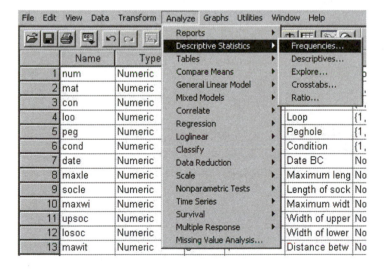

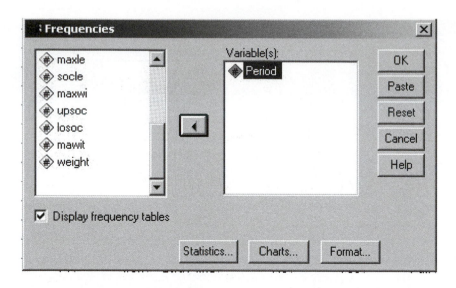

Date(Period)

		Frequency	Percent	Valid Percent	Cumulative Percent
Valid	Late	12	30.0	30.0	30.0
	Middle	11	27.5	27.5	57.5
	Early	17	42.5	42.5	100.0
	Total	40	100.0	100.0	

This shows that there are 17 'Early' spears. Note that this output shows that the three new values for Period have had Value labels attached as explained earlier in this section. (1 = Late etc).

14.2 Chapter 2: No packages used.

14.3 Chapter 3: Tabular and pictorial Display
To produce a simple frequency table in SPSS for the variable <COND> as in Table 3.2 use Analyse/Descriptive Statistics/Frequencies

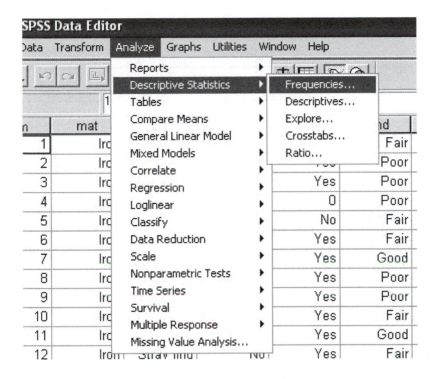

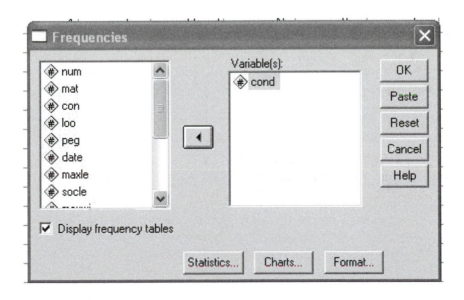

Condition

		Frequency	Percent	Valid Percent	Cumulative Percent
Valid	Excellent	8	20.0	20.0	20.0
	Good	18	45.0	45.0	65.0
	Fair	9	22.5	22.5	87.5
	Poor	5	12.5	12.5	100.0
	Total	40	100.0	100.0	

To make a bivariate table as in Table 3.4

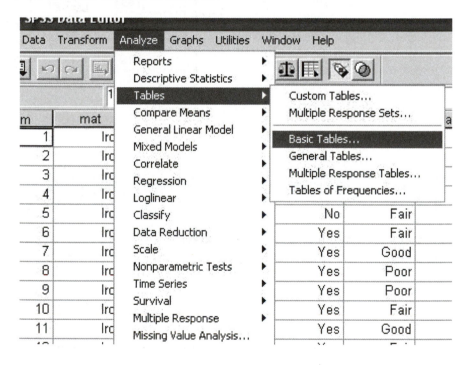

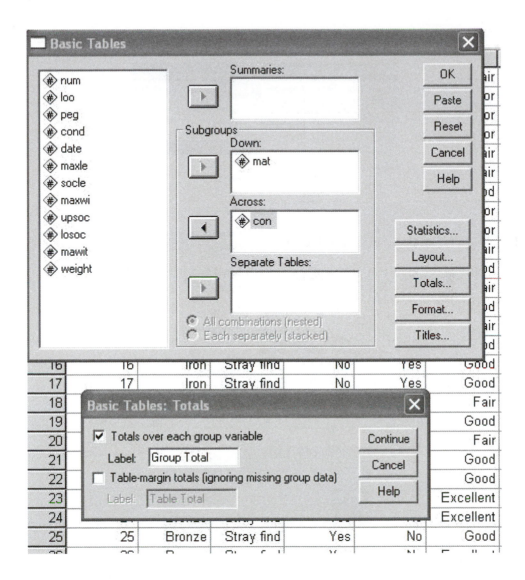

		Context			
		Stray find	Settlement	Burial	Group Total
Material	Bronze	19	1		20
	Iron	8	5	7	20
Group Total		27	6	7	40

By clicking **Statistics** various cell contents can be obtained as in Table 3.5

A simple bar chart like Figure 3.1 is produced by: Analyse/Graphs/Bar/Simple/Define

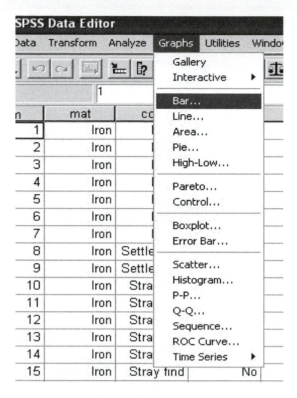

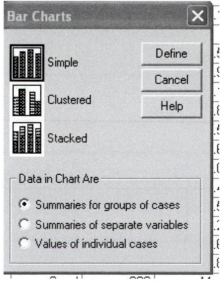

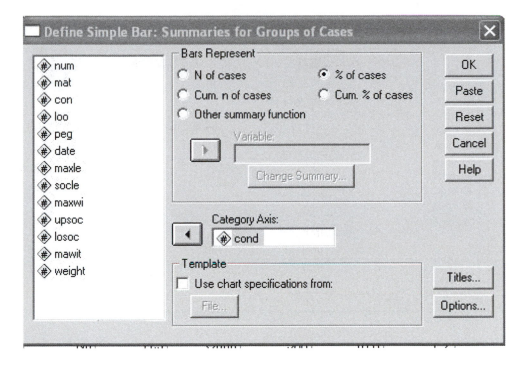

Once the chart has been created by SPSS it may be edited. Simply double click on the chart and this takes you to the chart editor. Here colours can be changed, titles edited, annotations made, axes altered etc. Try experimenting. When finished choose **Close** to return to the output file.

To reproduce Figure 3.2, which is a clustered bar chart use:

Graphs/Bar/Clustered/Define

and put the variables <COND> and <MAT> into the dialogue box as shown below:

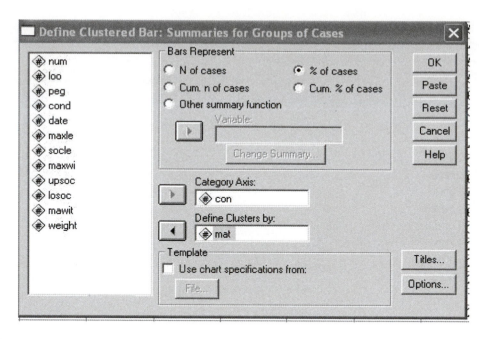

Histograms are produced using Graphs/Histogram and can be edited by double clicking on them to alter the axes or class widths.

For scatterplots such as Figure 3.11, use Graphs/Scatter/Simple/Define and put <MAXWI> as the Y axis and <MAXLE> as the X axis with <MAT> as the marker variable, as shown below.

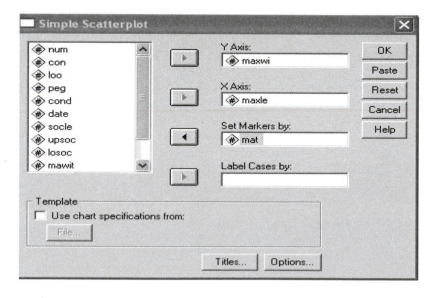

174

14.4 and 14.5 Chapters 4 and 5: Measures of position and variability
To obtain descriptive statistics for a variable use
Analyse/Descriptive Statistics/Descriptives
and put as many variables as you want into the window. This will produce output like
that shown below.

	N	Minimum	Max	Mean	Std. Deviation
Maximum length (cm)	38	10.2	72.4	20.674	11.4362
Maximum width (cm)	39	1.8	6.4	4.187	1.3213
Valid N (listwise)	38				

This command has several options and the ability to save standardized versions of the
variables.

Finally for these two chapters, Boxplots are drawn using Graph/Boxplot.

14.6 Chapter 6: No packages used.

14.7 Chapter 7: No packages used.

14.8 Chapter 8: Tests of Difference
All three t-tests and their non-parametric equivalents are available in SPSS. For the t-
tests use Analyse/Compare Means/ and then choose the appropriate test. To test if the
mean width of lower socket is different between bronze spears with and without pegs,
assuming normality, we should use an independent samples t–test, after first selecting
only Bronze spears. First select from the data only Bronze spears i.e. those for which
Material = 1. Do this using Data/Select Cases and then filling in the If option, as
shown below.

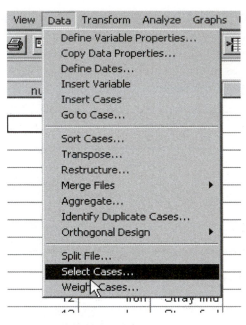

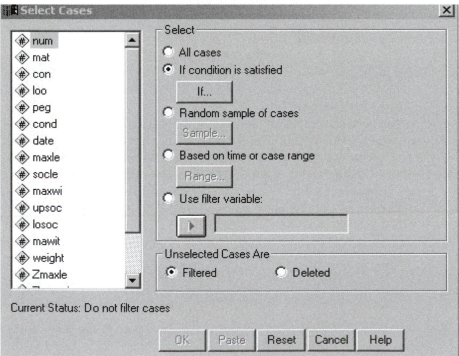

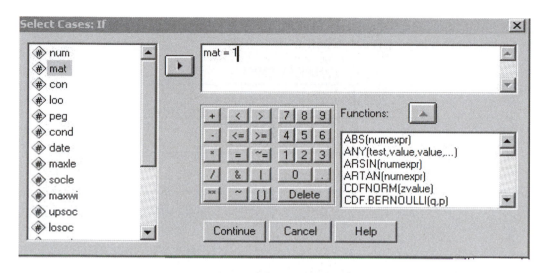

Then choose the appropriate t-test as below.

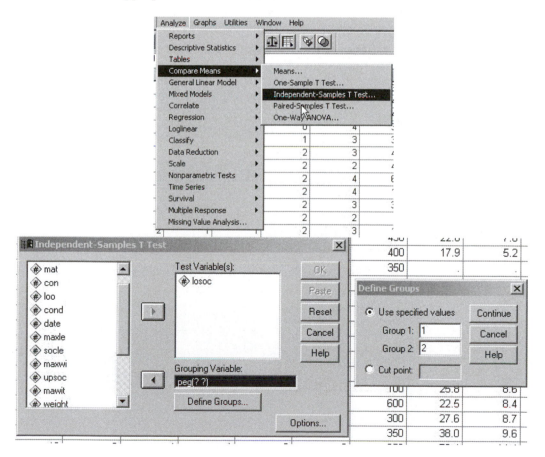

Here is the output confirming that there is significant evidence that bronze spears with a peghole have a larger lower socket.

Group Statistics

	Peghole	N	Mean	Std. Deviation	Std. Error Mean
Width of lower socket (cm)	No	10	2.010	.4067	.1286
	Yes	10	2.350	.2068	.0654

Independent Samples Test

		Levene's Test for quality of Variance		t-test for Equality of Means						
							Mean	Std. Error	95% Confidence Interval of the Difference	
		F	Sig.	t	df	Sig. (2-tailed)	Difference	Difference	Lower	Upper
Width of low socket (cm)	Equal variance assumed	8.267	.010	-2.356	18	.030	-.3400	.1443	-.6432	-.0368
	Equal variance not assumed			-2.356	13.362	.034	-.3400	.1443	-.6509	-.0291

If normality cannot be assumed than the Mann-Whitney test is appropriate. This can be found using Analyse/Nonparametric Tests/Independent Samples as shown below.

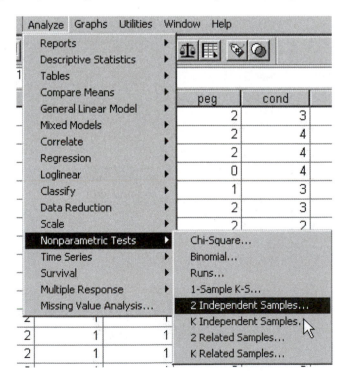

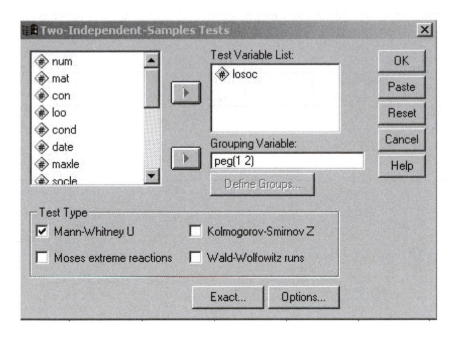

The output shown below confirms that there is significant evidence of a difference.

Ranks

	Peghole	N	Mean Rank	Sum of Ranks
Width of lower socket (cm)	No	10	7.85	78.50
	Yes	10	13.15	131.50
	Total	20		

Test Statistics[b]

	Width of lower socket (cm)
Mann-Whitney U	23.500
Wilcoxon W	78.500
Z	-2.018
Asymp. Sig. (2-tailed)	.044
Exact Sig. [2*(1-tailed Sig.)]	.043[a]

a. Not corrected for ties.

b. Grouping Variable: Peghole

14.9 Chapter 9: Tests of Distribution

To carry out a Kolmogorov-Smirnov test select the variable and the distribution to be tested.

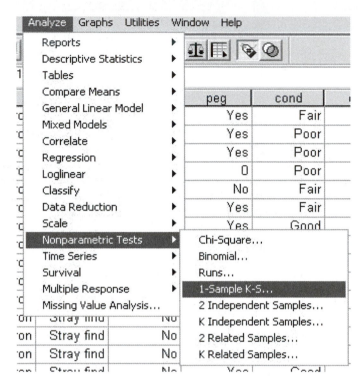

To compare a distribution in a histogram to a normal distribution just click the display normal curve check box as below.

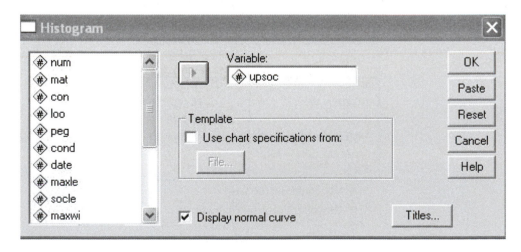

To create a normal probability plot as in Figure 9.6 use Graphs/P-P/ as below.

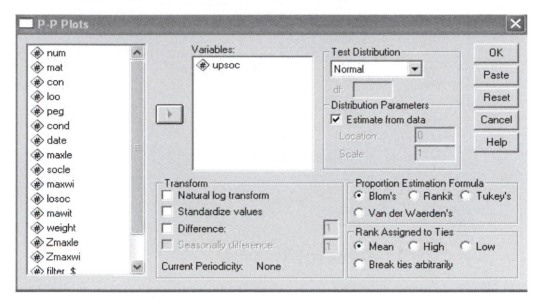

14.10 Chapter 10: Measures of Association – correlation.
The first step is usually to draw a scatter plot of the two variables under investigation as explained in section 14.3. To calculate a correlation coefficient to measure the correlation between maximum length and maximum width use Analyse/Correlate/Bivariate as shown below.

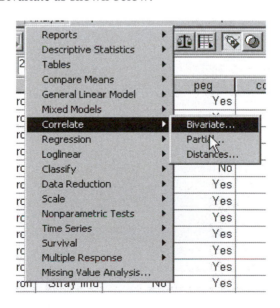

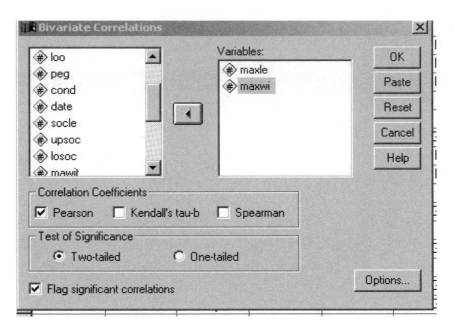

Note that here Pearson or p.m.c.c. is chosen and significance is measured. To calculate the correlation coefficient just for Bronze spears, first select from the data only Bronze spears i.e. those for which Material = 1. Do this using Data/Select Cases and then filling in the If option, as shown below.

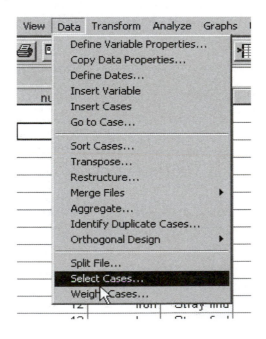

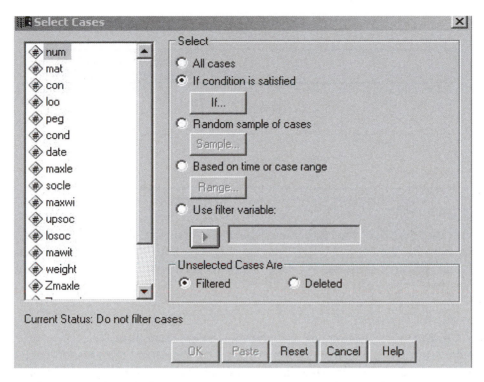

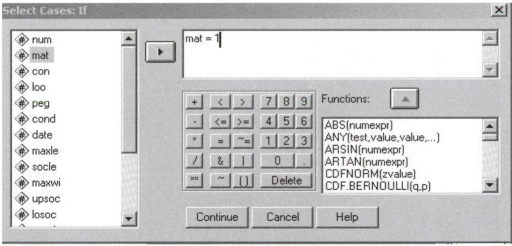

The results for this are as below, showing that the correlation between <MAXLE> and <MAXLE> is, as expected, +1.0, whilst the correlation between <MAXLE> and <MAXWI> is 0.674 and this is significantly different from 0.

Correlations

		Maximum length (cm)	Maximum width (cm)
Maximum length (cm)	Pearson Correlation	1	.674**
	Sig. (2-tailed)		.001
	N	20	20
Maximum width (cm)	Pearson Correlation	.674**	1
	Sig. (2-tailed)	.001	
	N	20	20

**. Correlation is significant at the 0.01 level (2-tailed).

If you want to measure the correlation between several variables then simply put a list of variables into the Correlate/Bivariate variables box and all possible coefficients will be given. Try it but keep the list short otherwise the output table will be too large to read easily.

14.11 Chapter 11: Measures of Association – categorical data

Consider reproducing the analysis from Chapter 11 measuring the association between <MAT> and <DATE> (Period). The first step is to transform the variable <DATE> into a new variable with three values, as was explained in 14.1. Then use Analyse/Descriptive Statistics/Crosstabs as shown below:

File	Edit	View	Data	Transform	Analyze	Graphs	Utilities	Window	Help

	num	mat		
1	1	Irc	Reports ▶	Fair
2	2	Irc	Descriptive Statistics ▶ Frequencies...	Poor
3	3	Irc	Tables ▶ Descriptives...	Poor
4	4	Irc	Compare Means ▶ Explore...	Poor
5	5	Irc	General Linear Model ▶ Crosstabs...	Fair
6	6	Irc	Mixed Models ▶ Ratio...	Fair
7	7	Irc	Correlate ▶ Yes	Good
8	8	Irc	Regression ▶ Yes	Poor
9	9	Irc	Loglinear ▶ Yes	Poor
10	10	Irc	Classify ▶ No	Fair
11	11	Irc	Data Reduction ▶ Yes	Good
12	12	Iron	Yes	Fair

In the Crosstabs dialogue box choose material and period as shown below:

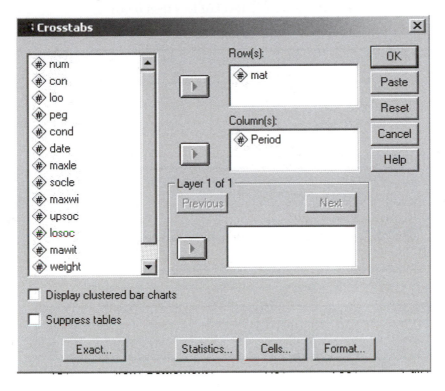

After choosing the two variables choose Statistics and then choose Chi-square as shown next:

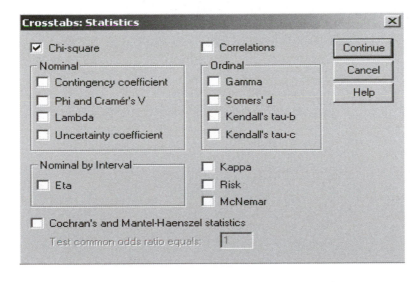

The resulting output below confirms the result in Chapter 11 with Chi-square (Pearson Chi-Square) = 31.27 and a significance level of less then 0.001

Chi-Square Tests

	Value	df	Asymp. Sig. (2-sided)
Pearson Chi-Square	31.273[a]	2	.000
Likelihood Ratio	42.561	2	.000
Linear-by-Linear Association	28.898	1	.000
N of Valid Cases	40		

a. 0 cells (.0%) have expected count less than 5. The minimum expected count is 5.50.

Material * Date(Period) Crosstabulation

Count

		Date(Period)			Total
		Late	Middle	Early	
Material	Bronze	0	3	17	20
	Iron	12	8	0	20
Total		12	11	17	40

Example 2 (tau-c). To find and test tau-c for the same problem repeat the previous steps but at the Statistics stage choose tau-c instead of Chi-square (you could of course choose both).

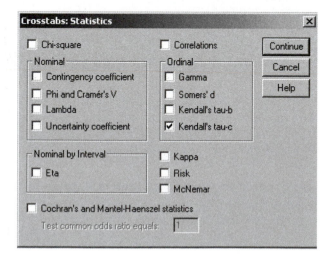

This produces the following output and again the earlier result is confirmed. Tau-c = −0.94 and is significant at the 0.1% level.

Symmetric Measures

		Value	Asymp. Std. Error^a	Approx. T^b	Approx. Sig.
Ordinal by Ordinal	Kendall's tau-c	-.940	.036	-26.172	.000
N of Valid Cases		40			

a. Not assuming the null hypothesis.

b. Using the asymptotic standard error assuming the null hypothesis.

14.12 Chapter 12: Multivariate analysis

The most versatile cluster analysis is Hierarchical Cluster analysis obtained in SPSS via Analyse/Classify/Hierarchical Cluster, as shown below.

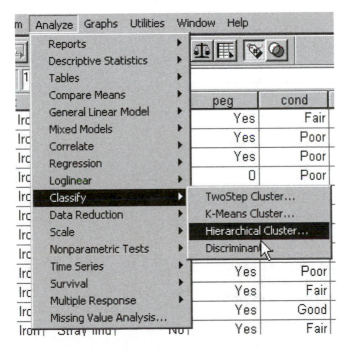

First choose the variables to use and any other choices such as which method, Saving cluster membership and plots. These are shown below for Between Groups linkage and Squared Euclidean distance, but many different options are available. Try a few!

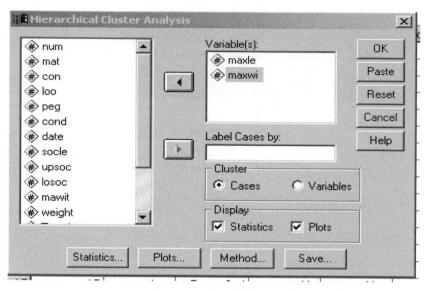

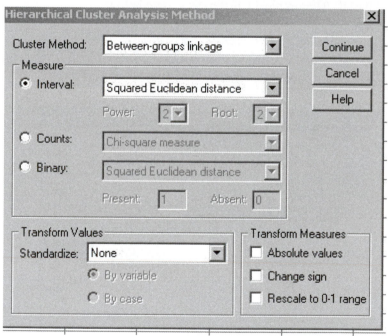

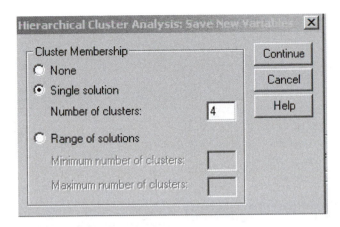

A new variable will be created called <CLU4_1> which will contain one of the four numbers 1, 2, 3 or 4. This variable can then be used as the marker for a scatterplot to produce Figure 12.4.

To produce the dendrogram shown in Figure 12.7 select the Plots box and tick Dendrogram as below.

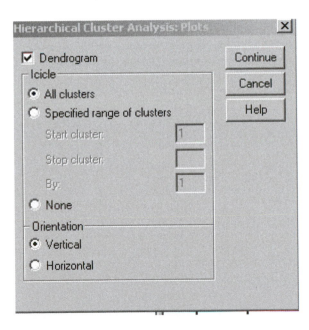

Correspondence Analysis is found under Analyse/Data Reduction/Correspondence Analysis as shown below.

Analyze	Graphs	Utilities	Window	Help

		Zmaxle	Zmaxwi
Reports ►		-.72346	-.444
Descriptive Statistics ►		.16844	.085
Tables ►		-.24254	-.065
Compare Means ►			
General Linear Model ►		-.33872	1.144
Mixed Models ►			
Correlate ►			
Regression ►			
Loglinear ►			
Classify ►			
Data Reduction ►	Factor...		
Scale ►	Correspondence Analysis...		
Nonparametric Tests ►	Optimal Scaling...		
Time Series ►		.15970	1.523
Survival ►		-.32998	-.444
Multiple Response ►		-.13761	-.065
Missing Value Analysis...		.44825	.388

After choosing the two variables <COND> and <CON> the range of values for each of these categorical variables must be Inputted and Updated as shown below.

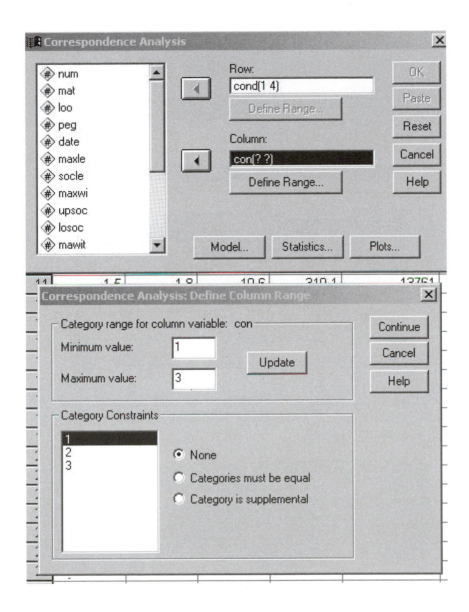

Multiple Regression can be found at Analyse/Regression/Linear as shown below.

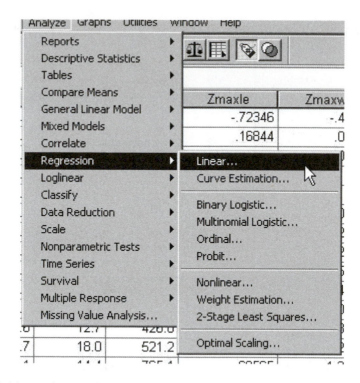

Put the variable to be predicted, <MAXLE> into the dependent box and all the independent variables into the lower box. The output is considerable but you should find Table 12.3 towards the end.

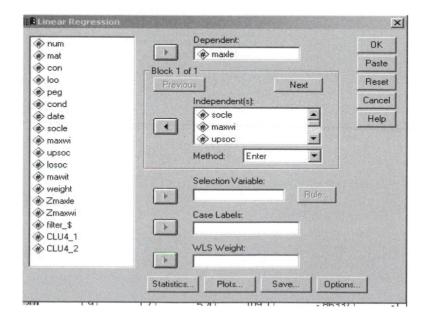

Discriminant Analysis is found at Analyse/Classify/Discriminant as shown below.

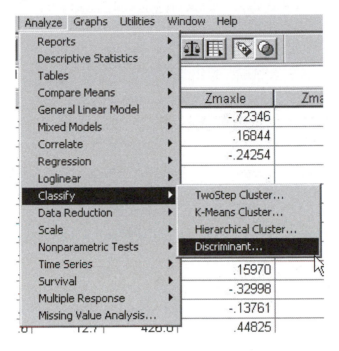

The variable to be discriminated goes as the grouping variable together with the range of values and the list of variables to be used goes in the lower box, as shown below:

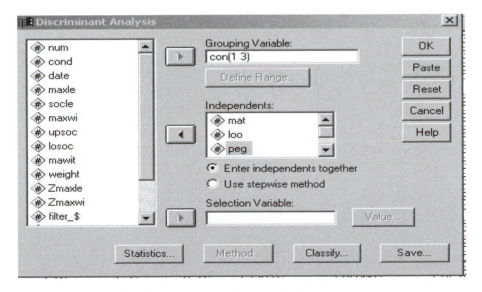

To get the summary table shown in Table 12.5 select the Classify button and then tick the Summary table box as shown below. If you only have a few cases the Casewise results produces interesting results.

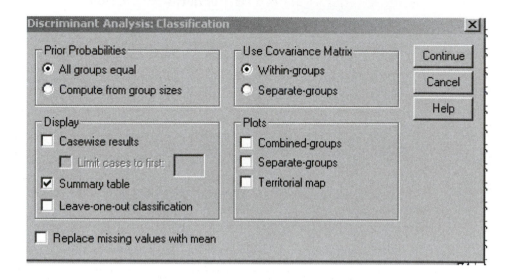

APPENDIX – STATISTICAL TABLES

Table A: Random digits from a uniform distribution

72310	28527	47920	03378	08262
38788	65902	90095	22211	32726
48561	37822	62026	76367	90792
70200	27857	53322	45953	49117
75046	82217	65261	44240	39736
80863	77208	57723	30061	67079
07997	51118	15396	57707	84932
99667	89856	24525	13416	16633
58515	32133	65621	76979	79189
14396	16670	02686	22432	98757
99564	83762	35741	04079	44780
45667	70403	67625	09915	97572
08424	00497	53172	39336	96605
53008	62075	46616	17100	75803
26039	59406	26995	38739	75527
54869	25779	74446	42446	41008
58648	22463	05816	05771	26005
31129	07955	26972	21362	50600
91128	94388	71554	70268	25001
91165	98579	44276	83549	25157
95747	22509	34550	43689	44697
68511	13664	18736	61146	87183
63925	07968	41997	43347	97969
90723	95988	49668	18383	46298
40548	98627	08504	97928	87352
68529	28517	62999	41082	19066

Table B: Percentage points of the t-distribution

d.f.	TWO SIDED TESTS					d.f.
	10%	5%	2%	1%	0.1%	
1	6.31	12.7	31.82	63.70	637.00	1
2	2.92	4.3	6.96	9.92	31.60	2
3	2.35	3.18	4.54	5.84	12.90	3
4	2.13	2.78	3.75	4.60	8.61	4
5	2.01	2.57	3.36	4.03	6.86	5
6	1.94	2.45	3.14	3.71	5.96	6
7	1.89	2.36	3.00	3.50	5.40	7
8	1.86	2.31	2.90	3.36	5.04	8
9	1.83	2.26	2.82	3.25	4.78	9
10	1.81	2.23	2.76	3.17	4.59	10
11	1.80	2.20	2.72	3.11	4.44	11
12	1.78	2.18	2.68	3.05	4.32	12
13	1.77	2.16	2.65	3.01	4.22	13
14	1.76	2.14	2.62	2.98	4.14	14
15	1.75	2.13	2.60	2.95	4.07	15
16	1.75	2.12	2.58	2.92	4.01	16
17	1.74	2.11	2.57	2.90	3.96	17
18	1.73	2.10	2.55	2.88	3.92	18
19	1.73	2.09	2.54	2.86	3.88	19
20	1.72	2.09	2.53	2.85	3.85	20
21	1.72	2.08	2.52	2.83	3.82	21
22	1.72	2.07	2.51	2.82	3.79	22
23	1.71	2.07	2.50	2.81	3.77	23
24	1.71	2.06	2.49	2.80	3.74	24
25	1.71	2.06	2.48	2.79	3.72	25
26	1.71	2.06	2.48	2.78	3.71	26
27	1.70	2.05	2.47	2.77	3.69	27
28	1.70	2.05	2.47	2.76	3.67	28
29	1.70	2.05	2.46	2.76	3.66	29
30	1.70	2.04	2.46	2.75	3.65	30
40	1.68	2.02	2.42	2.70	3.55	40
60	1.67	2.00	2.39	2.66	3.46	60
120	1.66	1.98	2.36	2.62	3.37	120
∞	1.64	1.96	2.33	2.58	3.29	∞
	5%	2.5%	1%	0.5%	0.05%	
d.f.	ONE SIDED TESTS					d.f.

Table C: 5% points of the F distribution

d.f.	1	2	3	4	5	6	7	8	9	10	12	15	20	30	60	120	∞
1	161	199	216	225	230	234	237	239	240	242	244	246	248	250	252	253	254.3
2	18.5	19.0	19.2	19.2	19.3	19.3	19.3	19.4	19.4	19.4	19.4	19.4	19.4	19.5	19.5	19.5	19 2
3	10.13	9.55	9.28	9.12	9.01	8.94	8.89	8.85	8.81	8.79	8.74	8.70	8.66	8.62	8.57	8.55	8.53
4	7.71	6.94	6.59	6.39	6.26	6.16	6.09	6.04	6.00	5.96	5.91	5.86	5.80	5.75	5.69	5.66	5.63
5	6.61	5.79	5.41	5.19	5.05	4.95	4.88	4.82	4.77	4.74	4.68	4.62	4.56	4.50	4.43	4.40	4.36
6	5.99	5.14	4.76	4.53	4.39	4.28	4.21	4.15	4.10	4.06	4.00	3.94	3.87	3.81	3.74	3.70	3.67
7	5.59	4.74	4.35	4.12	3.97	3.87	3.79	3.73	3.68	3.64	3.57	3.51	3.44	3.38	3.30	3.27	3.23
8	5.32	4.46	4.07	3.84	3.69	3.58	3.50	3.44	3.39	3.35	3.28	3.22	3.15	3.08	3.01	2.97	2.93
9	5.12	4.26	3.86	3.63	3.48	3.37	3.29	3.23	3.18	3.14	3.07	3.01	2.94	2.86	2.79	2.75	2.71
10	4.96	4.10	3.71	3.48	3.33	3.22	3.14	3.07	3.02	2.98	2.91	2.85	2.77	2.70	2.62	2.58	2.54
11	4.84	3.98	3.59	3.36	3.20	3.09	3.01	2.95	2.90	2.85	2.79	2.72	2.65	2.57	2.49	2.45	2.40
12	4.75	3.89	3.49	3.26	3.11	3.00	2.91	2.85	2.80	2.75	2.69	2.62	2.54	2.47	2.38	2.34	2.30
13	4.67	3.81	3.41	3.18	3.03	2.92	2.83	2.77	2.71	2.67	2.60	2.53	2.46	2.38	2.30	2.25	2.21
14	4.60	3.74	3.34	3.11	2.96	2.85	2.76	2.70	2.65	2.60	2.53	2.46	2.39	2.31	2.22	2.18	2.13
15	4.54	3.68	3.29	3.06	2.90	2.79	2.71	2.64	2.59	2.54	2.48	2.40	2.33	2.25	2.16	2.11	2.07
16	4.49	3.63	3.24	3.01	2.85	2.74	2.66	2.59	2.54	2.49	2.42	2.35	2.28	2.19	2.11	2.06	2.01
17	4.45	3.59	3.20	2.96	2.81	2.70	2.61	2.55	2.49	2.45	2.38	2.31	2.23	2.15	2.06	2.01	1.96
18	4.41	3.55	3.16	2.93	2.77	2.66	2.58	2.51	2.46	2.41	2.34	2.27	2.19	2.11	2.02	1.97	1.92
19	4.38	3.52	3.13	2.90	2.74	2.63	2.54	2.48	2.42	2.38	2.31	2.23	2.16	2.07	1.98	1.93	1.88
20	4.35	3.49	3.10	2.87	2.71	2.60	2.51	2.45	2.39	2.35	2.28	2.20	2.12	2.04	1.95	1.90	1.84
21	4.32	3.47	3.07	2.84	2.68	2.57	2.49	2.42	2.37	2.32	2.25	2.18	2.10	2.01	1.92	1.87	1.81
22	4.30	3.44	3.05	2.82	2.66	2.55	2.46	2.40	2.34	2.30	2.23	2.15	2.07	1.98	1.89	1.84	1.78
23	4.28	3.42	3.03	2.80	2.64	2.53	2.44	2.37	2.32	2.27	2.20	2.13	2.05	1.96	1.86	1.81	1.76
24	4.26	3.40	3.01	2.78	2.62	2.51	2.42	2.36	2.30	2.25	2.18	2.11	2.03	1.94	1.84	1.79	1.73
25	4.24	3.39	2.99	2.76	2.60	2.49	2.40	2.34	2.28	2.24	2.16	2.09	2.01	1.92	1.82	1.77	1.71
26	4.23	3.37	2.98	2.74	2.59	2.47	2.39	2.32	2.27	2.22	2.15	2.07	1.99	1.90	1.80	1.75	1.69
27	4.21	3.35	2.96	2.73	2.57	2.46	2.37	2.31	2.25	2.20	2.13	2.06	1.97	1.88	1.79	1.73	1.67
28	4.20	3.34	2.95	2.71	2.56	2.45	2.36	2.29	2.24	2.19	2.12	2.04	1.96	1.87	1.77	1.71	1.65
29	4.18	3.33	2.93	2.70	2.55	2.43	2.35	2.28	2.22	2.18	2.10	2.03	1.94	1.85	1.75	1.70	1.64
30	4.17	3.32	2.92	2.69	2.53	2.42	2.33	2.27	2.21	2.16	2.09	2.01	1.93	1.84	1.74	1.68	1.61
40	4.08	3.23	2.84	2.61	2.45	2.34	2.25	2.18	2.12	2.08	2.00	1.92	1.84	1.74	1.64	1.58	1.51
60	4.00	3.15	2.76	2.53	2.37	2.25	2.17	2.10	2.04	1.99	1.92	1.84	1.75	1.65	1.53	1.47	1.39
120	3.92	3.07	2.68	2.45	2.29	2.17	2.09	2.02	1.96	1.91	1.83	1.75	1.66	1.55	1.43	1.35	1.25
∞	3.84	3.00	2.60	2.37	2.21	2.10	2.01	1.94	1.88	1.83	1.75	1.67	1.57	1.46	1.32	1.22	1.00

Tables D and E: Kolmogorov-Smirnov single sample test

D				E			
Uniform and other completely specified distributions				**Normal distribution**			
n	10%	5%	1%	n	10%	5%	1%
1	95.0	97.5	99.5	1	-	-	-
2	77.6	84.2	92.9	2	-	-	-
3	63.6	70.8	82.9	3	36.7	37.6	38.3
4	56.5	32.4	73.4	4	34.5	37.5	41.3
5	50.9	56.3	66.9	5	31.9	34.3	39.7
6	46.8	51.9	61.7	6	29.7	32.3	37.1
7	43.6	48.3	57.6	7	28.0	30.4	35.1
8	41.0	45.4	54.2	8	26.5	28.8	33.3
9	38.8	43.0	51.3	9	25.2	27.4	31.7
10	36.9	40.9	48.9	10	24.1	26.2	30.4
11	35.2	39.1	46.8	11	23.1	25.1	26.2
12	33.8	37.5	44.9	12	22.3	24.2	28.1
13	32.6	36.1	43.3	13	21.5	23.4	27.1
14	31.4	34.9	41.8	14	20.8	22.6	26.3
15	30.4	33.8	40.4	15	20.1	21.9	25.5
16	29.5	32.7	39.2	16	19.5	21.3	24.8
17	28.6	31.8	38.1	17	19.0	20.7	24.1
18	27.9	30.9	37.1	18	18.5	20.2	23.5
19	27.1	30.1	36.1	19	18.1	19.7	22.9
20	26.5	29.4	35.2	20	17.7	19.2	22.4
21	25.9	28.7	34.4	21	17.3	18.8	21.9
22	25.3	28.1	33.7	22	16.9	18.4	21.4
23	24.8	24.5	33.0	23	16.5	18.0	21.0
24	24.2	26.9	32.3	24	16.2	17.6	20.6
25	23.8	26.4	31.7	25	15.9	17.3	20.2
26	23.3	25.9	31.1	26	15.6	17.0	19.8
27	22.9	25.4	30.5	27	15.3	16.7	19.5
28	22.5	25.0	30.0	28	15.1	16.4	19.2
29	22.1	24.6	29.5	29	14.8	16.2	18.8
30	21.8	24.2	29.0	30	14.6	15.9	18.6
31	21.4	23.8	28.5	31	14.4	15.7	18.3
32	21.1	23.4	28.1	32	14.2	15.4	18.0
33	20.8	23.1	27.7	33	14.0	15.2	17.7
34	20.5	22.7	27.3	34	13.8	15.0	17.5
35	20.2	22.4	26.9	35	13.6	14.8	17.3
36	19.9	22.1	26.5	36	13.4	14.6	17.0
37	19.7	21.8	26.2	37	13.2	14.4	16.8
38	19.4	21.5	25.8	38	13.0	14.2	16.6
39	19.2	21.3	25.5	39	12.9	14.0	16.4
40	18.9	21.0	25.2	40	12.7	13.9	16.2
41	18.7	20.8	24.9	41	12.6	13.7	16.0
42	18.5	20.5	24.6	42	12.4	13.5	15.8
43	18.3	20.3	24.3	43	12.3	13.4	15.6
44	18.1	20.1	24.1	44	12.2	13.3	15.5
45	17.9	19.8	23.8	45	12.0	13.1	15.3
46	17.7	19.6	23.5	46	11.9	13.0	15.1
47	17.5	19.4	23.3	47	11.8	12.8	15.0
48	17.3	19.2	23.1	48	11.7	12.7	14.8
49	17.2	19.0	22.8	49	11.6	12.6	14.7
50	17.0	18.8	22.6	50	11.4	12.5	14.5
55	16.2	18.0	21.6	55	10.9	11.9	13.9
60	15.5	17.2	20.7	60	10.5	11.4	13.3
65	14.9	16.6	19.9	65	10.1	11.0	12.8
70	14.4	16.0	19.2	70	9.7	10.6	12.4
75	13.9	15.4	18.5	75	9.4	10.3	12.0
80	13.5	15.0	18.0	80	9.1	9.9	11.6
85	13.1	14.5	17.4	85	8.9	9.6	11.3
90	12.7	14.1	16.9	90	8.6	9.4	10.9
95	12.4	13.8	16.5	95	8.4	9.1	10.7
100	12.1	13.4	16.1	100	8.2	8.9	10.4

For large values of n use:

	5%	1%
Uniform	$135.8/\sqrt{n}$	$162.8/\sqrt{n}$
Normal	$89.9/\sqrt{n}$	$105.0/\sqrt{n}$

Table F: Kolmogorov-Smirnov two sample test

n_A	n_B	5%	1%
5	5	25	25
5	6	24	30
5	7	28	35
5	8	30	35
5	9	35	40
5	10	40	45
5	11	39	45
5	12	43	50
5	13	45	52
5	14	46	56
5	15	55	60
5	16	54	64
5	17	55	68
5	18	60	70
5	19	61	71
5	20	65	80
5	21	69	80
5	22	70	83
5	23	72	87
5	24	76	90
5	25	80	95
6	6	30	36
6	7	30	36
6	8	34	40
6	9	39	45
6	10	40	48
6	11	43	54
6	12	48	60
6	13	52	60
6	14	54	64
6	15	57	69
6	16	60	72
6	17	62	73
6	18	72	84
6	19	70	83
6	20	72	88
6	21	75	90
6	22	78	92
6	23	80	97
6	24	90	102
6	25	88	107
7	7	42	42
7	8	40	48
7	9	42	49
7	10	46	53
7	11	48	59
7	12	53	60
7	13	56	65
7	14	63	77
7	15	62	75
7	16	64	77
7	17	68	84
7	18	72	87

n_A	n_B	5%	1%
7	19	76	91
7	20	79	93
7	21	91	105
7	22	84	103
7	23	89	108
7	24	92	112
7	25	97	115
8	8	48	56
8	9	46	55
8	10	48	60
8	11	53	64
8	12	60	68
8	13	62	72
8	14	64	76
8	15	67	81
8	16	80	88
8	17	77	88
8	18	80	94
8	19	82	98
8	20	88	104
8	21	89	107
8	22	94	112
8	23	98	115
8	24	104	128
8	25	104	125
9	9	54	63
9	10	53	63
9	11	59	70
9	12	63	75
9	13	65	78
9	14	70	84
9	15	75	90
9	16	78	94
9	17	82	99
9	18	90	108
9	19	89	107
9	20	93	111
9	21	99	117
9	22	101	122
9	23	106	126
9	24	111	132
9	25	114	135
10	10	70	80
10	11	60	77
10	12	66	80
10	13	70	84
10	14	74	90
10	15	80	100
10	16	84	100
10	17	89	106
10	18	92	108
10	19	94	113

n_A	n_B	5%	1%
10	20	110	130
10	21	105	126
10	22	108	130
10	23	114	137
10	24	118	140
10	25	125	150
11	11	77	88
11	12	72	86
11	13	75	91
11	14	82	96
11	15	84	102
11	16	89	106
11	17	93	110
11	18	97	118
11	19	102	122
11	20	107	127
11	21	112	134
11	22	121	143
11	23	119	142
11	24	124	150
11	25	129	154
12	12	84	96
12	13	81	95
12	14	86	104
12	15	93	108
12	16	96	116
12	17	100	119
12	18	108	126
12	19	108	130
12	20	116	140
12	21	120	141
12	22	124	148
12	23	125	149
12	24	144	168
12	25	138	165
13	13	91	117
13	14	89	104
13	15	96	115
13	16	101	121
13	17	105	127
13	18	110	131
13	19	114	138
13	20	120	143
13	21	126	150
13	22	130	156
13	24	140	166
13	25	145	172
14	14	112	126
14	15	98	123
14	16	106	126
14	17	111	134

n_A	n_B	5%	1%
14	18	116	140
14	19	121	148
14	20	126	152
14	21	140	161
14	22	138	164
14	23	142	170
14	24	146	176
14	25	150	182
15	15	120	135
15	16	114	133
15	17	116	142
15	18	127	152
15	19	127	152
15	20	135	160
15	21	138	168
15	22	144	173
15	23	149	179
15	24	156	186
15	25	160	195
16	16	128	160
16	17	124	143
16	18	128	154
16	19	133	160
16	20	140	168
16	21	145	173
16	22	150	180
16	23	157	187
16	24	168	200
16	25	167	199
17	17	136	170
17	18	133	164
17	19	141	166
17	20	146	175
17	21	151	180
17	22	157	187
17	23	163	196
17	24	168	203
17	25	173	207
18	18	162	180
18	19	145	176
18	20	152	182
18	21	159	189
18	22	164	196
18	23	170	204
18	24	180	216
18	25	180	216
19	19	171	190
19	20	160	187
19	21	163	199
19	22	169	204
19	23	177	209

n_A	n_B	5%	1%
19	24	183	218
19	25	187	224
20	20	180	220
20	21	173	199
20	22	176	212
20	23	184	219
20	24	192	228
20	25	200	235
21	21	189	231
21	22	183	223
21	23	189	227
21	24	198	237
21	25	202	244
22	22	198	242
22	23	194	237
22	24	204	242
22	25	209	250
23	23	230	253
23	24	205	249
23	25	216	262
24	24	240	288
24	25	225	262
25	25	250	300
26	26	260	313
27	27	270	324
28	28	308	364
29	29	319	377
30	30	330	390
31	31	341	403
32	32	352	416
33	33	396	462
34	34	408	476
35	35	420	490
36	36	432	504
37	37	444	518
38	38	456	570
39	39	468	585
40	40	520	600
41	41	533	615
42	42	546	630
43	43	559	688
44	44	572	704
45	45	585	720
46	46	644	736
47	47	658	752
48	48	672	768
49	49	686	833
50	50	700	850

For large values of n_A and n_B use:

$$5\% = 1.358\sqrt{n_A n_B (n_A + n_B)} \qquad 1\% = 1.628\sqrt{n_A n_B (n_A + n_B)}$$

Table G: Critical values for correlation coefficient (PMCC)

n	5%	1%		n	5%	1%			n	5%	1%
1	-	-		31	0.355	0.456			61	0.252	0.327
2	-	-		32	0.349	0.449			62	0.25	0.325
3	0.997	-		33	0.344	0.442			63	0.248	0.322
4	0.95	0.99		34	0.339	0.436			64	0.246	0.32
5	0.878	0.959		35	0.334	0.43			65	0.244	0.317
6	0.811	0.917		36	0.329	0.424			66	0.242	0.315
7	0.755	0.875		37	0.325	0.418			67	0.24	0.313
8	0.707	0.834		38	0.32	0.413			68	0.239	0.31
9	0.666	0.798		39	0.316	0.408			69	0.237	0.308
10	0.632	0.765		40	0.312	0.403			70	0.235	0.306
11	0.602	0.735		41	0.308	0.398			71	0.234	0.304
12	0.576	0.708		42	0.304	0.393			72	0.232	0.302
13	0.553	0.684		43	0.301	0.389			73	0.23	0.3
14	0.532	0.661		44	0.297	0.384			74	0.229	0.298
15	0.514	0.641		45	0.294	0.38			75	0.227	0.296
16	0.497	0.623		46	0.291	0.376			76	0.226	0.294
17	0.482	0.606		47	0.288	0.372			77	0.224	0.292
18	0.468	0.59		48	0.285	0.368			78	0.223	0.29
19	0.456	0.575		49	0.282	0.365			79	0.221	0.288
20	0.444	0.561		50	0.279	0.361			80	0.22	0.286
21	0.433	0.549		51	0.276	0.358			82	0.217	0.283
22	0.423	0.537		52	0.273	0.354			84	0.215	0.28
23	0.413	0.526		53	0.271	0.351			86	0.212	0.276
24	0.404	0.515		54	0.268	0.348			88	0.21	0.273
25	0.396	0.505		55	0.266	0.345			90	0.207	0.27
26	0.388	0.496		56	0.263	0.342			92	0.205	0.267
27	0.381	0.467		57	0.261	0.339			94	0.203	0.265
28	0.374	0.479		58	0.259	0.336			96	0.201	0.261
29	0.367	0.471		59	0.256	0.333			98	0.199	0.259
30	0.361	0.463		60	0.254	0.33			100	0.197	0.257

Table H: Critical values for Spearmans's rank correlation coefficient

n	5%	1%	n	5%	1%	n	5%	1%
1	-	-	31	0.356	0.459	61	0.252	0.329
2	-	-	32	0.350	0.452	62	0.250	0.326
3	-	-	33	0.345	0.446	63	0.248	0.323
4			34	0.340	0.439	64	0.246	0.321
5			35	0.335	0.433	65	0.244	0.319
6	0.886	1.00	36	0.330	0.427	66	0.243	0.316
7	0.786	0.929	37	0.325	0.421	67	0.241	0.314
8	0.738	0.881	38	0.321	0.416	68	0.239	0.311
9	0.700	0.833	39	0.317	0.41	69	0.237	0.309
10	0.649	0.794	40	0.313	0.405	70	0.235	0.307
11	0.618	0.755	41	0.309	0.400	71	0.234	0.305
12	0.587	0.727	42	0.305	0.396	72	0.232	0.303
13	0.56	0.703	43	0.301	0.391	73	0.231	0.301
14	0.539	0.679	44	0.298	0.387	74	0.229	0.299
15	0.521	0.654	45	0.295	0.382	75	0.227	0.297
16	0.503	0.635	46	0.291	0.378	76	0.226	0.295
17	0.488	0.618	47	0.288	0.374	77	0.224	0.293
18	0.472	0.600	48	0.285	0.370	78	0.223	0.291
19	0.460	0.584	49	0.282	0.366	79	0.222	0.289
20	0.447	0.570	50	0.279	0.363	80	0.220	0.287
21	0.436	0.556	51	0.276	0.359	82	0.217	0.284
22	0.425	0.544	52	0.274	0.356	84	0.215	0.280
23	0.416	0.532	53	0.271	0.352	86	0.212	0.277
24	0.407	0.521	54	0.269	0.349	88	0.210	0.274
25	0.398	0.511	55	0.266	0.346	90	0.207	0.271
26	0.390	0.501	56	0.264	0.343	92	0.205	0.268
27	0.383	0.492	57	0.261	0.340	94	0.203	0.265
28	0.376	0.483	58	0.259	0.337	96	0.201	0.262
29	0.369	0.475	59	0.257	0.334	98	0.199	0.260
30	0.362	0.467	60	0.255	0.331	100	0.197	0.257

Table I: Percentage points of the χ^2 distribution

d.f.	10%	5%	1%	0.1%	d.f.
1	2.71	3.84	6.63	10.8	1
2	4.61	5.99	9.21	13.8	2
3	6.25	7.81	11.3	16.3	3
4	7.78	9.49	13.3	18.5	4
5	9.24	11.1	15.1	20.5	5
6	10.6	12.6	16.8	22.5	6
7	12.0	14.1	18.5	24.3	7
8	13.4	15.5	20.1	26.1	8
9	14.7	16.9	21.7	27.9	9
10	16.0	18.3	23.2	29.6	10
11	17.3	19.7	24.7	31.3	11
12	18.5	21.0	26.2	32.9	12
13	19.8	22.4	27.7	34.5	13
14	21.1	23.7	29.1	36.1	14
15	22.3	25.0	30.6	27.7	15
16	23.5	26.3	32.0	39.3	16
17	24.8	27.6	33.4	40.8	17
18	26.0	28.9	34.8	42.3	18
19	27.2	30.1	36.2	43.8	19
20	28.4	31.4	37.6	45.3	20
21	29.6	32.7	38.9	46.8	21
22	30.8	33.9	40.3	48.3	22
23	32.0	35.2	41.6	49.7	23
24	33.2	36.4	43.0	51.2	24
25	34.4	37.7	44.3	52.6	25
26	35.6	38.9	45.6	54.1	26
27	36.7	40.1	47.0	55.5	27
28	37.9	41.3	48.3	56.9	28
29	39.1	42.6	49.6	58.3	29
30	40.3	43.8	50.9	59.7	30

INDEX